I0121285

Charles Wesley Kyle

Forest leaves and other poems

Charles Wesley Kyle

Forest leaves and other poems

ISBN/EAN: 9783743328846

Manufactured in Europe, USA, Canada, Australia, Japa

Cover: Foto ©Thomas Meinert / pixelio.de

Manufactured and distributed by brebook publishing software
(www.brebook.com)

Charles Wesley Kyle

Forest leaves and other poems

Charles Wesley Kyle

FOREST LEAVES

AND OTHER POEMS

BY

CHARLES WESLEY KYLE

HANDSOMELY ILLUSTRATED

For every aspiration of the Soul
Which thou wouldst better know and satisfy,
Go to the fount of knowledge — Nature's fount —
Receive from out her hand the truth unsoiled,
And thou shalt find a rest naught else can give.

SAN FRANCISCO

D. S. STANLEY & COMPANY, PRINTERS AND PUBLISHERS

1894

CONTENTS

FOREST LEAVES.

CONTENTS.

DIALECT POEMS.

BLOSSOMS AND BRIARS.

PATRIOTIC AND MISCELLANEOUS POEMS.

ILLUSTRATIONS.

TO ALMA KYLE-HUFFMAN.

SISTER, whose love of Nature taught
Mine own to love the mountains grand;
For whom in youth I plucked and brought
The first bright flowers of all the land;
My first bouquet of "Forest Leaves,"
Culled from fair Mother Nature's breast,
I bring to thee, while my heart grieves
To think they are not fairest — best.

C. W. K.

PROEM.

Come, let us sail, with what success we may,
To-morrow may be still a cloudy day;
Perchance the waves of yon great untried sea
May be more smooth than they appear to be;
And yon great breakers little dangers hold,
If we be firmly brave, and calmly bold.
I've heard it oft, that literary sharks
Love most to pounce upon dull, timid marks;
For, like the vultures, they exulting soar
O'er lifeless wrecks cast high upon the shore.
Their guns shoot just as far, roar just the same,
Be katydids or elephants their game!
Old sages wrote, and I believe it still,
That half the battle lieth in the will.
No doubt that thousands would, but somehow don't,
And other thousands could, but then they won't.
So if this voyage ever is to be,
Why, we must sail it, risk the untried sea;
And if our boat a dull illusion prove,
The troubled dream will soon be safely o'er;
Far better this, than never dare to move,
And rotting lie upon the lifeless shore.
So lend a hand, all willing friends — here goes,
With kind regards to you — deuce take our foes.

THE ANTHEM OF THE HILLS.

THE ANTHEM OF THE HILLS.

I climbed amid the granite spires and domes
Of Nature's temples. The scene was morning—
Early morn — for yet the shroud of night
Was folded over all the nearer hills,
And that strange and most impressive silence
Of expectancy, which rules the moments
That precede momentous revelations,
Pressed heavily upon fair Nature's lips.
Night's mantle ruled the sight, save one pale view,
Which to the eye appeared as if the moon,
New-born, had fallen from the skies and caught,
With points downturned, upon a mountain's brow
To eastward.

The twinkling stars shone brightly,
But, as I gazed, their gold to silver turned,
And Night, with noiseless winging, moved away.
Beyond the mountain peaks Morn's heralds gleamed,
Their brilliant lances piercing all the sky.
The world awoke: hard by, from out the pines,
A blue jay called; robins a-wing gave key
To all the leafy woodland's matin choir.
The mellow murmur of the ocean's waves
Came floating faintly from afar, and there
The wakened sea-fowl, screaming, rose and fanned,
With measured stroke, the slowly whitening air.
A light and balmy breeze strayed softly o'er
The organ of the pines, to try the keys;
The mountain streams murmured a louder strain,
And all the instruments were found attuned.

A ray of gold shot o'er the mountain's brow;
It was the leader's magic signal wand,
And then, clearly but softly, there arose,
In unison, two voicings from the glen —
A duet, sung by mountain-brook and bird!
So sweet, the winds ceased winging and gave ear,
Rendering all the listening throng complete.
Again the leader's bright wand waved apace,
And other voices from the feathered throng
Joined in the song. A gleam! and all was still.
The low winds softly played an interlude,
And then the black-winged oriole, master
Of all the mountain choir, a solo gave,
So pure and sweet in melody, each note
Proclaimed the very soul of perfect song,
Which, floating on the air, there wove complete
A psalm of joy all inexpressible!
Then came the choral of the full-voiced throng,
And there was heard such bursts of harmony
As stirred the fibers of the human heart,
And drew from out emotion's deepest well
The pearly gems of purest joy! the while,
Trembling with ecstasy, my very soul
Leaned out to catch the meaning of the song.

Adorned with robes of light, the mountains round,
And all the rocky glens, re-echoed, o'er and o'er again,
The song. The tall pines trembled; every key
Responding to the touches of the wind,
While ever and anon the charming scenes
Of variegated cloud and changing light
Were shifted to and fro by hands unseen.
These draperies, clinging to peak and sky,
Were blendings of pearl-gray, of blue and gold,
More beautiful in color and design
Than the imagination can conceive,
Or skill of greatest master can portray.
The perfect music swelling from that throng
Sounded a pæan of triumphal joy;
When, lo! the god of day, mounting the sky
With dazzling splendors, ushered in his rule.

A CALIFORNIA AUTUMN.

The hills are bronzed with Summer's dying breath;
The sunlight sifting through the haze,
Of half-formed cloud, which, like a dream
But half-remembered, folds the days
In robes of softened orange gleam,
Befitting Summer's universal death.

Down from the hills the rivers murmur low,
As on their journeys to the sea
They would their notes of song defer,
And in low-spoken tones agree
With spirit of this sepulcher,
Where gentle winds are winging soft and slow.

Down by the sea the billows of the tide
Beat softly 'gainst the rock-ribbed shore,
Appealing with their lips of white,
In voicings of a muffled roar,
Alike through hours of day and night,
For peace and rest which ever is denied.

Beyond the stubble-fields, the water-oaks
And manzanita tangles lie
In the arroyos of the hills;
And holding Summer's hands, defy
The encroachment of Autumn's ills,
Emeralding the bronze which Nature cloaks.

The mountain tops are robed in sombre blue;
The forest trees let fall their gold,
Which carpets deeply all the ground,
Or by the winds is gently rolled
In many a pyramidal mound,
Which Time cements with falling rain and dew.

Like a bronzed pilgrim, weary with the strife
Of battling with the elements,
Sweet Summer falls with moaning sigh,
And with her call to rest contents
Her, 'neath the Autumn's robes to lie,
And slowly yield the brightness of her life.

THE GOLDEN GATE.

"Make way! make way!" from the ocean wide,
Was heard the voice of its restless tide,
As the dashing waves, with ceaseless roar,
Knocked at the gates of the rocky shore.

"Give back, we pray, and let us in,
Where we may rest from the ocean's din;
The toil of ages has been our fate —
One hour of slumber to compensate!"

Thus pleaded the waves with sob and moan,
'Til they touched the heart of the cold, gray stone,
And the shore was moved by the ocean's fate,
And unlocked the bars of the Golden-Gate.

Then the waves rushed in, and, since that day,
Have found a haven within the bay,
Where the voice of children and breath of flowers
Have rendered sweet their restful hours.

"Make way! make way!" comes another cry,
Filling the earth and the azure sky,
From that ocean strange, whose billows be
The troubled souls of humanity!

With their wistful pleadings o'er and o'er,
They knock at the gates of a voiceless shore;
The boundless shores of their narrow sea,
Unknown, unmeasured — Eternity!

Though the shores be voiceless and tempests rage,
Hope sends a gleam for an anchorage;
And the tired souls gather of strength to wait
'Til the bars shall drop from the Pearly Gate.

AMBITION.

Could I catch the soul of the flowers and birds,
Of the woodlands wild, where the Dryads sing;
Could I place the song of the winds in words,
As hither and thither they softly wing;
Could I lose my soul in the bright blue sky,
Then I think I would be content to die.

THE SUNLIGHT ON THE HILLS.

The mountains are aflame with light
(The sunlight rests upon the hills),
Their snowy crowns a brilliant sight,
From which come flashing crystal rills.
The day wears on toward its close,
Night's early gloom the valley fills;
While silence tends to sweet repose,
The sunlight fades from off the hills.

Up, up the rough and rocky steep
(Above the gloom-enshrouded hills)
The evening shadows softly creep,
Stealing the lances from the rills,
Hushing the voices of the earth —
The grinding of the water-mills,
The song of birds, the shouts of mirth,
With which the world the daylight fills.

The mountain heights now glow with flame,
(The sun is faded from the hills),
Their beauty rare eludes a name,
And every heart with worship fills.
Befitting thrones for gods they seem —
Omnipotence their grandeur wills;
Their regal robes with splendors gleam
Above the drap'ries of the hills.

Now, up the mountain, twilight steals
(Night settles on the lower hills),
And to the shepherd boy reveals
The hour to pipe his evening trills.
Adown the winding mountain way
The music every crevice fills,
Proclaiming that the god of day
Has died amid the western hills.

THE WOOD-NYMPH.

Silence! tread softly, this spot is enchanted:
For, just over there in the pines,
A Wood-nymph is drinking the wines
That are brewed in the cups
Of the Johnny-jump-ups
And the fresh golden dandelions.

Look! now she is drinking from the white lily,
Which gracefully bends to her lips,
As of its pure brewing she sips;
Her wealth of dark tresses,
The coy breeze caresses —
A beauty naught else can eclipse.

See! now she is looking through the green leafage,
To that mossy bank over there,
Half yielding, I see, is her air.
Behold, now she passes,
Athwart the green grasses—
A queen, every whit, I declare.

Now she reclines on the sweet velvet mosses—
A lacing umbrageous above—
To sleep and to dream of her love;
While the wild bird and bee
Woos the dream-god to see
That refreshing her rest shall prove.

Come away, come away, no mortal should dare,
His presence to ever make known—
Let her rest in peace all alone—
For all Wood-nymphs are pure
And they cannot endure
A mortal's approach to their throne.

CONTENTMENT.

In the mountains grand, where the white river rushes,
    Foaming and singing with a light, joyous bound;
Where the wild roses creep with their crimson blushes,
    And pour from their flagons sweet perfume around;
There the honey-bees, o'er the fresh, blooming clover,
    With the dragon-flies hum a low, drowsy tune—
Under the white peaks that lean in and watch over,
    Are green vales that cradle the sweet joys of June.

To rare cloud-forms kissed, the white sea-mist there dapples
    The fathomless arch of the sweet Summer sky;
In the deep, cooling shades grow the mango apples,
    And slow, winging winds breath a gentle sigh.
And there, at the foot of the great snow-topped mountains,
    Filling the deep bowl of each pine-circled urn
From the liquid wealth of their vast, snowy fountains,
    The calm, smiling lakes to the blue heavens turn.

In the broad, rich valleys the green fields a-tossing,
All heavily topped with rich kernels of gold;
Billowed and flecked by the cloud-shadows crossing,
As Summer, wind-steeded, is over them rolled.
The kine in the meadows at midday are resting,
"Contentment" they picture; field, meadow and stream,
With turtle-dove silent, in water-oak nesting,
Draped with gray purple—enchanting day-dream!

The gold-fingered willows bend low as to listen
To tale which the mountain brooks cheerfully tell;
The blooms of the dog-wood, star-shaped, purely glisten,
While rings for the fairies the lovely blue-bell.
Azaleas and buckeyes enrich the wood's dressing,
The blackberries' crimson besplashes the glen;
The robin, the charms of the wildwoods confessing,
Pours forth sweetest praise, while all echo "Amen!"

ON THE BAY.

Soft, cloudless skies o'er-arched the hills and sea;
The Autumn day, one dream of solitude;
The air a shimmering veil of gold and blue,
Fallen from Summer's slow-departing form
For that short interval of quietude
Which waits on Winter's coming. Dreamy scene.
Breathed every sound a note of melody.
The snow-white swan afloat the swelling wave,
And ships, with great wings spread, move out to sea.
With oarlocks drawn we drift but with the tide.

The sun sinks toward the sea; long shadows throw
Athwart the bay their unsubstantial forms.
The sea-gulls and the swans, with measured stroke,
Now fan their way, each to his chosen rest.
Out from the East, Night spreads her sable wings,
And in the West is lost the gold of day.
No discord marks the change. Peace ruleth still;
From out the sombre arch of Autumn's night,
A thousand scintillating stars shine on—
God's sentinels, which watch while dreams the world.

THE MOUNTAIN SHORE.

There's a beautiful land toward the evening of day,
    Where the mountains majestically rise;
Where the murmuring fountains are ever at play
    'Neath the softest and bluest of skies;
Where sweet Summer, serene, in the valleys below,
    Lingers on one bright scene of delight;
Where the mountains, rich clothed with an emerald glow,
    Are a matchlessly beautiful sight.

Where the voice of the streamlets breaks ever in song
    Of rich melody pure and complete,
As they rush from the mountains through valleys along,
    Which lead down to the sea at their feet;
Where the stars of the night with such brilliancy gleam,
    Through the soft, misty mantle of shade;
Like the eyes of the angels of heaven they seem
    In their robes of deep purple arrayed.

Where the faintest of winds ever sigh o'er the land,
    Chanting low through the evergreen pine
The sweetest of music—an æolian band,
    Every breath a sweet chord all divine.
And the sun, as its beams slowly die in the West,
    Charms the eye with a beautiful sight—
Blushing crimson and gold on the mountain's green crest,
    As it kisses them fondly good-night.

Oh, come to these mountains, ye children of men,
    And all these grand temples behold;
Once seen, you can ever recall them again,
    As the leaves of your mem'ry unfold;
These rough, rocky peaks, towering up to the sky,
    These valleys, soft velvet with sod,
Are sceneries grand which all time will defy,
    For their painter and sculptor is God.

THE PEACE OF NATURE.

Gushing from the green-capped mountains,
Where the larks and daisies meet,
Over shells and mossy pebbles,
Making music low and sweet,
Strays a laughing, silv'ry brooklet,
'Neath the pine and laurel's shade,
Bounding over terraced places,
Like some wand'ring Indian maid.
Changing ever, yet forever
Changeless in its form and tone,
Voicing Nature's love completest,
When unstartled and alone.

Thus preserve it for the future;
Marring not its virgin sod,
Where in beauty there is written
Message from the hand of God.
Let the wild birds mate and carol,
Safe from the destroyer's hand,
Where the raging seas are conquered
By the giants of the land.
Let one spot be left unbroken,
Where the toils of conflict cease,
And where Nature's soothing voices
Whisper to the weary: "Peace."

THE ROSE'S TOMB.

I saw a rose-vine slowly creep
Upward, along a mountain wall,
And, pausing not to rest or sleep,
It clambered onward up the steep,
Braving the dangers, one and all.

At last it reached the mountain's crest,
Where am'rous sunbeams kissed to bloom
The buds with which its life was blest;
Then plucked by Love was laid on breast
Of lady fair. How sweet a tomb!

INVERNESS.

The blooming hills of Inverness,
How bright they gleam,
How fresh they seem,
In robings rich of Summer dress!
With beauty's wealth of grace they bless
The mind with joy—the heart caress;
In every flower
A wondrous power,
Waking the love I now confess
For thee, my own fair Inverness.

From sea a veiling light of mist
Is drifting o'er
Thy hilly shore,
Kissed by the sun to amethyst.
I could not if I would resist
Thy subtle power. How deeply missed
Thy shore and sea?
In memory
Thou wilt be veiled in sorrow's mist,
Tinted by love to amethyst.

GOLD LAKE.

Cradled amid the rocky spires,
Which form the crown
Of earth; where mountains pierce the skies,
And look far down
From regions where the drifted snow
Beats back the warmth of Summer's glow,
And answer gives but in the flow
Of crystal rills,
To all earth's pleadings from below,
Where Summer wills.

Gold Lake! the gem of waters pure,
By sunbeams kissed
(Amid the rocks which time endure)
To amethyst,
Lies, like a precious pearl of worth,
A jewel sacred to the earth,

Which hath been guarded since the birth
Of mountains grand;
When ocean's universal girth,
Gave up the land.

Serene and calm thy waters lie
Constant through years;
Receiving from the changeful sky
Her smiles and tears;
Vain were the hope that there should be
In human hearts, save dreamily,
Reflection of thy constancy,
Until a calm
Like thine shall come the heart to free
By death's sure balm.

First to receive the morning's light,
Whose tim'rous ray
Invades the shadows of the night
To herald day.
Last to receive the ray of sun,
Whose fading glimmers, one by one,
Proclaim his work and journey done,
As, in the West,
He slowly dies. Thus be begun
Our final rest.

SONG TO THE SIERRAS.

Ye monuments of earth's unmeasured splendor,
Piercing the heaven's unfathomed vault of blue,
From Winter falling to the flower-land tender,
Which smiles to you!

Ye lofty spires and granite domes uplifted,
Beyond the feeble power of man to climb;
The snows of ages on your proud forms drifted,
Vision sublime!

Voicings of God! His power and force unmeasured!
Beyond all mortal scope to comprehend
The beauties, by thy mighty giants treasured
From end to end.

Thy revelations brook not words confining;
    The measure of our power to think and feel,
Prevents our grasping all of His consigning
        Thou wouldst reveal.

Cathedrals grand! sculptured by force of ages;
    Unheeding thou the constant flight of time;
The grandest thought appearing on earth's pages,
        Lore all sublime!

The anthem which your mighty waters thunder,
    Through glaciered peaks, where never man hath trod,
Cause angel hosts to meditate and wonder,
        At throne of God!

Your placid lakes! mirrors of heaven unnumbered!
    Framed with the snows and unconsuming fires;
How long, fair gems, have ye thus sweetly slumbered
        Amid these spires?

Your matchless forms sermons divine are preaching,
    From glaciered peak to foot-beverdured sod;
The fragrant flowers, within thy vales, are teaching
        The way to God.

Your lovely brooks, which tinkle to the measure
    Of granite keys, o'er which they leap and play,
Voice, constantly, a melody of pleasure,
        Both night and day.

The pine-clad vales, begemmed with bloom and beauty,
    To every sense of head and heart appeal;
With stately grace perform their highest duty—
        God to reveal.

Immortal beauty! grandeur all supernal!
    From awe-inspiring summit to the rose,
Thy voicings—all thy teachings—are eternal,
        Though Time should close.

Imperial sculpturings of God's true glory,
    So long as thou shalt point unto the sky,
Telling to man the grand immortal story,
        Hope cannot die.

DIVINITY OF NATURE.

Who that has felt the solemn power
Of mountain groves of pine,
For even one short, fleeting hour,
Can doubt a power divine?

Is it but winds and mountains high,
But trees and grass and flowers;
But snowy peaks and azure sky,
That so enchant these bowers?

Why should the soul that comes in touch
With Nature's work alone
Be drawn to better thoughts so much,
If soul-power be unknown?

'Tis not the trees and mountains grand,
The sea, the flowers, the sky;
They are but the Great Master's wand,
Drawing our thoughts on high.

The finer arts our spirits raise,
From grosser ties of earth;
In them is sung the sweetest praise
To Him who gave us birth.

WHEN THE DAY-GOD DIES.

The splashing of the fountains
And the murmur of the rills
In the royal, snow-capped mountains,
And the lower wooded hills,
Hush their tones almost to silence,
And a veil creeps o'er the skies,
As Time pauses for a moment
When the golden day-god dies.

AN AUTUMN IMPRESSION.

I stood in the hills when Autumn
Had painted them crisp and brown,
And saw the robes of the forest
Falling regretfully down—
At least the wavering motion
Of each gold and scarlet leaf
Seemed to me as if voicing
The soul of unmeasured grief.

The bare, blue arms of the buckeyes,
The gaunt, dead limbs of the pines,
Were full of sorrowful meaning—
As a heart when it hope resigns.
The wind, with a low intoning,
A requiem softly sung,
And mist, like of tears, was falling
As from heart of Nature wrung.

The grasses were dried and withered,
The song-birds had mostly fled ;
The flowers had long since been gathered,
And Summer lay cold and dead.
A funeral train was passing—
The mourners I seemed to hear—
Muffled and low was the sobbing,
Tear-stained the face of the year.

The notes of the wind grew louder,
And trembled each tiny spray ;
The skies overhead grew brighter,
And the mists were swept away.
The gold of the sunbeams falling
Changed the erstwhile mournful scene,
Until it appeared befitting
The throne of a royal queen.

The light in the West was gorgeous—
Most brilliant of all the day;
Kissing the forest-clad mountains,
And gilding each leaf and spray.
It seemed to me as a message :
That darkness and death and pain
Were steps in Life's great procession—
That all things should live again.

TO A ROBIN.

Thou merry herald of the Spring,
 Thy liquid notes, so pure and sweet,
Throughout the fields and orchards ring,
 Telling of Winter's sure retreat.

Fortelling birth of grass and flowers,
 Of springing corn and waving wheat—
All children of the sun and showers,
 That cometh forth the Spring to greet.

It must be that thy little breast
 Is warmed and cheered by love's sweet glow;
That thoughts of tiny eggs and nest
 Call forth thy sweet song's rippling flow.

Ah! robin, robin, would that I
 Might fly with free and careless wing,
To cold and storms I'd bid good-bye,
 And journey ever with the Spring.

A MAY MORNING IN THE WOOD.

All nature smiling fresh and glad,
    Bedecked as for a holiday,
In royal robes is richly clad,
    To welcome thee, sweet month of May.
The orchestra within the grove,
    Glad overtures is heard to play,
As all the grand processions move,
    Just at the peep of coming day.

The lark mounts up with cheering song,
    The linnets trill a roundelay ;
Then all join in a chorus strong
    To celebrate the birth of day.
The squirrel, creeping from his nest,
    Now gaily scampers o'er the ground,
Or, measures space from tree to tree—
    The acrobat—with fearless bound.

The mocking bird now takes his seat
    On topmost bough of tallest tree,
And every listening ear doth greet
    With sweetest notes of minstrelsy.
Then from low branch of tree hard by
    Comes floating a sweet voice of love ;
None more heart-touching 'neath the sky
    Than this soft note of turtle-dove.

The turkeys, from their lofty perch,
    Call "quit, quit, quit," then reach the ground,
And straightway they begin their search
    Till some secluded spot is found.
Perchance you see some tardy owl
    Drowsily winging home to bed ;
He seems half devil and half fowl,
    With wond'ring stare of hornèd head.

On spreading boughs of yonder oak
    Are pigeons feeding on its burrs;
The morn no sound from them awoke—
    They're Nature's silent worshipers.
A sudden flash from out the sky—
    A crash! and then a rumbling sound;
A hawk tells you the reason why
    The birds high circle, round and round.

From every leaf and blade of grass
    Depends a wealth of jewelry,
Which flashes brightly as we pass—
    Night's gift to Morning's revelry.
If you would chase away dull care,
    And Nature see in charming mood,
Rise with the lark and with me share
    Some pleasant morning in the wood.

LILIES.

Kissed by the sunshine,
    Fed by the dew,
None are so sweetly fair,
    Lilies, as you.
Pure as the morning air,
    When Summer's kiss
Wakens from slumbers pure
    Your loveliness.

Emblems of innocence,
    Queens of the field,
Fragrance no other flowers
    Like yours can yield.
All that is pure and fair,
    In all the earth,
The gods have given you,
    Sweet flowers, at birth.

AN ADMONITION.

When next I meet you at the club,
On trout to dine,
Pray do not give my faith the rub,
For as fish swim and are good grub,
When flanked with wine,
It cannot stand to hear about
Thy wondrous skill in luring trout
With rod and line.

Now mark it, friend, I do not say
Because, forsooth,
My faith some wavering may betray,
That you have not—in fact, alway,
From early youth,
Been kind to her—aye, kept your word
Bright as a warrior's gleaming sword,
Defending Truth !

But, pardon me, if it seems bold
In me to ask :
Do others' faith lay firmly hold
Upon this tale when it you've told?
And do they bask
Beneath that self-complacent smile?
And does it every doubt beguile—
A perfect mask?

You "cast," you say, full forty feet,
And lured a "rise"
Just where the alder bushes meet
The waters ; in that cool retreat
Where shadows lie
Upon the stream and still its roar,
Beneath a giant sycamore,
Which towers the sky?

AN ADMONITION.

Your "catch," you say, was seven pound,
And two foot three?
Well, well, it must be holy ground
Where such enormous trout are found.
The Banyan tree
No greater gift could e'er confer
Upon the heathen worshiper,
Than this to me.

Direct me to this sycamore,
I pray thee, friend,
That my poor faith you may restore,
I truthful deem you as of yore,
And no more lend
An ear to doubt, whene'er you speak;
Be henceforth strong, as now I'm weak,
Unto the end.

The oily lines you love to use
No doubt are fine,
But even oil you may abuse;
Oiled lines of speech can but amuse,
For false design
Reveals itself through every word,
And every oily tone that's heard
Is falsehood's sign.

So when you meet me next, my friend,
I truly wish
You graciously would strive to lend,
Your powers all thought to kindly tend
Away from fish;
I seriously bewail your fate,
You lie so easily of late
When trout's our dish!

THE WINDING EEL.

Ho, for the mountains green, that render
    The crystal streams with their snowy foam,
Which dash 'neath the sunlight's golden splendor,
    Where the "cut-throat" sports in its liquid home.
Where Peace like a spirit of comfort dwelling,
    O'er the troubled souls of the weary steal,
The charms of life to the heart revealing—
    Ho, for the banks of the winding Eel!

Where the blue skies arch the redwood's columns,
    That shelter the doe and her spotted fawn;
Where the crickets chirp, when the gloaming solemns
    The restful hours from the eve 'til dawn.
Where life's elixirs and rich ozone,
    Distilled by the pines, through the senses steal
On every wind of the mountains blown —
    Ho, for the banks of the winding Eel!

Ho, for a day of rest in the mountains,
    Away from the noise of the busy crowd;
Where voice of birds, of streams, and fountains
    Alone break the hush of Nature's shroud.
There by the banks of the river, flowing,
    To live again with the rod and reel;
The heart and cheek with pleasure glowing—
    Ho, for the banks of the winding Eel!

A camp in the glen, where the tall pines whisper,
    When touched by the wings of the morning winds,
And murmur sweetly a magical vesper,
    When day in the westward slowly declines.
There days are pleasure and nights are peace,
    Where joys of freedom the soul may feel,
And every trouble and care shall cease—
    Ho, for the banks of the winding Eel!

A NIGHT IN CAMP.

On the mountain's side where the redwoods, growing
Like columns, appear to support the sky;
Where crystal streams are forever flowing,
And Grandeur sits sponsor to Beauty nigh;
Where Nature tells her grandest story,
And lights the past with her magic lamp,
Flooding the scene in a blaze of glory,
We made our camp.

In a lovely dell, where the pines lean over
To catch the note of the streamlet's song—
That minstrel bard and mountain rover,
Which tireless sings for the mountain throng.
There, where the daylight first is sleeping,
And rest speaks peace to the heart's desire,
When the Gheber's god to the West was creeping,
We lit our fire.

No lamp had we, save the camp-fire glowing,
No need—for Nature supplied us all;
The lamps of Heaven, their light bestowing,
Shone through the curtain which Night let fall.
Night—so beautiful, weird and solemn,
Silent—yet list to the undertone!
Unbroken, save the glowing column
By camp-fire thrown.

How wierdly sweet are the mystic voices
Which throng and whisper amid the pines,
As sweet Nature silently rejoices
That Night on her bosom now reclines.
We lay us down to a peaceful slumber,
But Beauty uncurtains full oft the eye,
As Naiads dance to the measured number
Of crickets' cry.

A NIGHT IN CAMP

UNIV. OF
CALIFORNIA

The coyotes howl from the shrouded hollow,
The night-owls hoot from the trees near by,
While breezes quickly each other follow,
From woodland waking a mournful sigh.
The sight grows dim, on the ear the drumming
Of woodland calls now faintly creep,
A low refrain as of fairies humming—
We dream and sleep.

The morning wakes—an ashen finger
Plucks from the eastward a glowing star;
The shadows yet in the gulches linger,
But Night has fled from the hills afar.
The blue jays call, the robins twitter,
The gray squirrel barks from across the way;
The pearls of mist on the tree tops glitter—
Behold, 'tis day.

THE TRUTHFUL ANGLER.

A "rainbow" treasure in the stream,
Rose cautiously; my fondest dream
Ne'er pictured trout with brighter gleam
Of beauty rare;
He for my presence did not seem
A fig to care.

Slowly he swam up to my fly,
And looked it o'er with careful eye.
I trembled, I will not deny,
With angler's chill,
To see him drawing still more nigh
With studied will.

He paused and slowly waved a fin,
The liquid mirror just within.
Tempting as my besetting sin
He now appeared;
Would he defeat my hope to win?
I greatly feared.

A moth then fell upon the wave;
One flirt the finny gamester gave,
The morsel caught, then sank to lave
Deep in the pool.
The words I said no soul would save,
Nor keep it cool.

Ho, ho! Sir Trout, I thought, I'll see
If that's the game you play with me,
I'll wily, as you're wary, be,
And so I straight-
Way found a moth conveniently
To use for bait.

With cautious skill I cast my lure,
Feeling I'd tempt the "beauty" sure.
I had no waiting to endure,
For, quick as thought,
The trout, the insect to secure,
Had struck and caught.

He was so large, this famous trout,
That as I speak I fear a doubt
In strangers' minds may rise, about
His weight and size;
Fully two feet, from tail to snout,
Was this grand prize.

I speak the truth (God save my soul!)
He bent full double my light pole
And lashed the waters of that hole
To foam and spray;
Just as I thought I'd got control
He broke away!

Now to complete this truthful tale,
To speak aught else my heart would fail,
I did not swear and rave or wail.
Devoutly then
I simply whispered to the gale:
Amen! amen!

THE SUPREME MOMENT.

There are moments, to the sportsman,
 When the glow of pleasure thrills
Every nerve within his being,
 And forgotten are all ills.
It is when the sound that's loudest
 Is the beating of his heart,
And he fears his faintest breathing
 Will his noble quarry start.

Creeping through the rubus tangles,
 Lying low 'mid grass or fern,
Silently with caution moving,
 Whilst his nerves with longing burn;
When he feels defeat or vict'ry
 On his highest skill depends,
In the touching of the trigger,
 Which anticipation ends.

Whether on the plains or marshes,
 In the fields or mountains wild,
He becomes a changed new being,
 Nature's worshiper and child.
There his every sense is pitted
 'Gainst a foe of worthy steel,
Whether wielding gun or rifle,
 Or the tempered rod and reel.

There is something in one's nature,
 Since the day of Adam's fall,
Which finds pleasure in the moment
 Of the win-or-lose-it-all.
Who of all the sportsmen, truly,
 Would not half their crowning give
For the pleasures which bejewel
 Every moment we thus live?

THE FIRST DAY OF THE SEASON.

I.

LETTER FROM MR. TWELVEBORE TO MR. SIXTEENGAUGE.

"SAN FRANCISCO, Saturday.

"Your kind invitation, with some other half score,
Lies open before me. It troubles me sore
At not being able to accept of them all.
If convenient the dates, I could shoot all the fall!
It's too bad, confound it! but then I suppose
Some thorns there must be on the bush of each rose.
I hope you'll feel flattered, for yours I accept,
With a joy that leaves all of the others unwept;
Though, of course, I must write in response to each one
(God forgive me for lying when that task is done!)
And say to them all, 'I am sorry, yes, quite
Sorry (though filled with unmeasured delight!)
That a prior engagement (that lie's done before!
I'll use it, by Jove! for this scant dozen more)
Prevents an acceptance.' Then wind up my wail
By wishing them 'luck' on their first hunt for quail.
I'll be up on Friday, the earliest train
Will carry me, sure, through the sunshine or rain;
Our footsteps must press on the 'season's' threshold,
Be skies clear or cloudy, the winds warm or cold.
My setter, 'high class' he is called, I believe,
Is too —— blue-blooded. He will not retrieve.
So I'll have to fall back again on old Joe,
The Gordon, whom some have affirmed was too slow,
But I've found him ready and staunch to the last;
If you keep up all day you'll agree he is fast.
If the birds are one-half as thick as they say,
We'll have glorious shooting one week from to-day.
Everybody is going, there'll be quite a throng,
Until then, believe me, your friend. Now 'so long;'
I must go and get ready.
Please make
To your wife my respects.
Sincerely,
TWELVEBORE.
I'll break
This off here."

II.

After posting this letter, old Mr. Twelvebore
Lit his "briar-root," a thing he had oft done before.
As the blue wreaths curled upwards he pleasantly smiled,
Which certified clearly that all cares were beguiled,
Or, at least, were displaced for the moment. Alas!
That cares are immortal—but we'll let that pass.
"Egad! this is lucky, just think of it now,
I'm in for some shooting. I must not allow
My friend, Sixteengauge, any leaway, to brag
About bringing of feathers the most to the bag.
I must see to my weapon, and load up my shells
With shot that on quail most effectively tells.
My skill in wing-shooting I haven't forgot,
As for cobwebs of age, of course, that is 'rot;'
I'll prove it so, drat me, and I'll let him see
That strabismus has not laid its hold upon me,
Or aught that can hinder my shooting.
Let's see—
'The cover,' he writes, 'is as good as can be
Along the arroyos leading back from the sea.
That the quail are quite thick, indeed 'tis believed
That on this point no sportsman need e'er be deceived.
And the fields so inviting, they could not be more
To the heart of a sportsman.' I've heard that before,
And the fact I'll not question. All men, I believe,
Exchange Faith for Hope themselves to deceive
In all things, perchance, where Truth, if made known,
Their fond cherished idols would dash from their throne."

III.

How sweet are the musings we ever may find
In anticipation, provided, the kind
Are akin to the sportsman's. What sweet pleasures he
May call up by reflection. The land and the sea
Pour out for him freely their jewels of wealth,
Crowning all with the priceless boon of good health.
The sights that he sees to the vision are fair;
The air that he breathes is a poison to care;

The tramps that he takes make his blood fresh and pure,
And give to his system the strength to endure.
It oft has been proven that this line of sport
Refines soul and body in Nature's retort.
Then mark the time, sportsmen, one week from to-day,
From the office and counter you all may away
To the broad, open valley or deep, narrow vale,
In pursuit of the gamy and swift-flying quail.

QUEEN OF THE HILLS.

Hail, spirit of true poesy, divine!
The whirling reel, the floating gossamer line!
Upon the mountain lake or foaming stream,
Where golden kisses of the sunlight gleam,
With graceful stroke the tempting lure to fling,
Flecking the waters with their coloring,
Are subjects fit for breathings of thy grace,
For Beauty there reveals her charming face.

The violets of the hillside are her eyes,
Which to the azured heavens send replies,
While o'er her cheeks the warm rose-blushes steal,
And trailing vine and nodding fern reveal
The sweet enchantment of her presence rare;
For naught of earth can with this Queen compare,
For every charm and grace to her are lent
By reason of her sweet environment.

A cord of silver is the foaming stream,
Which winds from mountain top with flashing gleam,
Lacing the vestment of her bosom pure,
Holding the grass and moss and fern secure,
Singing, the while, a cadence soft and low,
Down to the sea from regal crest of snow,
Kissing the royal redwoods as they rest—
A boutonniere upon her lovely breast.

THE MUSIC OF THE REEL.

There is music in the woodland
When the matin breezes blow
Through the forest trees that shadow
The fresh river's rippling flow;
Where the golden sunbeams softly
Through the leafy branches steal,
And the angler's ear is gladened
By the whirring of the reel.

Do you love the mountain valleys?
Do you love afar to roam,
Where on rocks the mountain river
Beats its wavelets into foam?
Come with me then in the morning,
With your rod and boots and creel,
And we'll angle for the artists
That make music on the reel.

Up amid the peaks that glisten
With eternal robes of snow,
Which, kissed by warm sun, furnish
Life to shrub and flower below;
Where its waters laugh and gambol,
Shouting loud peel after peel,
We will wait, and watch, and listen
For the music of the reel.

There are players, skilled and finished,
In the art of music's school,
But none can play the instrument
Of the tribe within the pool.
Cast you flies upon the waters,
If the pleasure you would feel
Which is wakened by the music
Flowing from the spinning reel.

Now the winds, low through the branches,
With slow wingings softly steal,
And the striking of the artist
Now within the pool you feel.
Gently waken now, as echoes,
The soft touches of the breeze,
And the artist in the river
Strikes upon the piercing keys.

How the music hums and quavers!
Oh! the joyous thrill you feel,
As, awakened from its slumbers,
Sings with glee the whirling reel!
Joys there may be that will equal
Those, which thus, we all may feel,
But to me there's none that's better
Than the music of the reel.

BEAUTIES OF NATURE.

There is no beauty like the rose;
The lily, oh, how passing fair!
The violet all sweetness knows;
The mountain brook has not a care.

THE BURNING OF MT. TAMALPAIS.

All over the mountain, the seasons,
With Time's fleeting shuttle of hours,
Had woven a robing of beauty,
By aid of the sunshine and showers.
The grasses which covered the valleys,
The bright flowers which bloomed in the glen,
A paradise formed in the woodlands,
Secure from the presence of men.

Here grasses and flowers and fern leaves,
Rich mosses and wild vines that run
Out from the cool shaded places,
To drink in the light of the sun,
Displayed the fine skill of the artist,
Whose rich, indestructible mine
Yields patterns and colors unnumbered;
Perfection in work and design!

Rich forests of pine and of cedar,
Clothed all of the gorges with green,
While here and there oak leaves of scarlet,
With gold of the aspen were seen.
The smilings of Summer had ripened
The grasses which grew in the vales;
Dry twigs and dead branches had fallen
Where hurled by the strength of the gales.

All over the old rugged mountain,
A dream of security lay;
The waves sang a song of rejoicing,
The sky was unclouded that day.
When down on the mountain a serpent
Crept silently out from the dell;
Its writhing form hissing and growing;
Imbued with the spirit of hell.

This serpent of flame, in its anger,
    Fanned fierce by the breath of the wind,
Swept up through the valleys and gorges;
    About every object entwined,
Clasped rude the fair rose in its splendor,
    Which gladdened the eye with its bloom;
One touch, and its beauty was ashes,
    One breath, and the air was its tomb!

The demons of fire full of madness
    Swept on with white heat in their flame;
Unknown was the spirit of Pity,
    And Mercy? They knew not the name!
The song birds grew suddenly silent,
    As up from the valleys below
Was wafted the roar of the conflict,
    Beneath the black flag of the foe.

The wild stag afar the flame scented;
    Sprang up from the carpet of green,
And whistled a challenge, defiant,
    To the foe which as yet was unseen.
The startled doe tremblingly followed,
    The spotted fawn close by her side;
Ye gods! what a beautiful picture,
    As over the mountain they glide!

The mountain, denuded of beauty,
    Now stands as a great blackened tower;
A symbol alone in its sadness,
    Of sturdy, invincible power.
The future is brightened with promise,
    The sunshine, the mists, and the rain,
Will woo into life brighter beauties,
    Than those by fire demons slain.

All men are but twigs and crude branches,
    The source of the plant is unseen;
Aye, so is the fruit — e'en the blossom
    Is yet but suggested, I ween.
What lies in the new life, I wonder,
    The life which the future will bring?
What thoughts will then thrill to emotion,
    What songs will the future lips sing?

HAIL AND FAREWELL.

Do you hear those feeble footsteps,
    As the Old Man totters by?
Do you hear his labored breathing
    And his melancholy sigh?
'Tis the Old Year slowly dying,
    His remaining hours are few;
For him now the winds are sighing:
    Good-bye, 1892.

Listen! the blue-bells are ringing,
    And the lilies blow their horn;
Listen! the wild birds are singing,
    For another year is born!
The fresh grasses grow more greenly,
    Nature sounds a jubilee,
And the blue skies smile serenely:
    Welcome, 1893!

CALIFORNIA'S OLD YEAR.

The Old Year dies to-night!
Elsewhere, the robe of snowy white;
Elsewhere, the parian wreath and crown
The heavens let fall so lightly down;
But here, beside his bed of death,
Is perfumed breath.

The hills are bright, and sweet the air,
The flowers are springing everywhere;
The dear Old Year will find a tomb
Beneath fresh grass and banks of bloom;
His form the earth will sweetly fold
In green and gold.

THE AUTOGRAPH OF GOD.

The day was Summer's. All about me rose
The terraced peaks and domes of mountains grand.
The rushing river loudly roared and beat
Its crystal waters into milk-white foam,
Flinging them aloft in sparkling fountains
That, in sun or shade, revealed a beauty
All their own. I clambered along its banks,
Now the great mountains closed on either hand,
With but the river's foaming line between,
While from the mountains' steep and rugged walls,
Set in the lofty niches, here and there,
A stately pine or twisted cedar grew,
Unvisited, save by the fearless birds,
Where, unmolested, they could find a home,
Which Nature had reserved for them alone.
Beyond, the mountains wavered back apace,
And there was set a little verdured glen,
Grass-covered, and grown o'er with lordly pines,
While, on the other hand, the river's course,
Half-circling, beat against a mighty wall
Which rose until it towered the very skies,
A veritable king and sentinel!

The river laughed and leaped in torrents wild,
Winding its foaming form adown the gorge.
From sky-land, where the snows and clouds conjoined,
Gave to it life and whitened lips of song.
Lo! as I gazed, there came above its fount
A mountain of the sky, which rose in haste
And spread above the stream its darkened form.
The low winds, whispering softly through the pines
Now grew to louder tones, swaying the boughs
Until they lashed and intertwined their forms,
Brushing their spiral cones and needles green
From off their stems, and hurling them in showers
Upon the foaming river and the green,
With which the glen was carpeted.
The organ of the sky with grandeur rolled

In thrilling tones its music down the gorge,
And then across the bosom of the cloud
The brilliant lightning traced its crooked way.
When, like a dazzling sheet of pearls, the rain
Unrolled from cloud to peak, a brilliant scroll,
On which, in colors indescribable,
Appeared, written with golden pencil of the sun,
The fresh and dazzling autograph of God!

EVENING IN THE HILLS.

Softly Night's mantle drapes the distant hills
And lies in darker folds within the vales;
Like silver cords the foaming mountain rills
In muffled voicings tell the woodland tales.

The crimson pencil of the dying sun
Paints weirdly all the mountain tops and sky;
Then bids good-bye to peaks, one after one,
Which slowly fade from sight of mortal eye.

The tall pines on the lofty mountain side
Blend slowly in one solid phalanx dark;
The shadows from about still nearer glide
And halt but at the camp-fire's blazing mark.

Strange voices fill the earth and all the air;
Night's children all about us dance and sing;
Their Queen is Conqueror! they all declare,
More potent than the day's most gorgeous King.

THE HONEST WORSHIPER.

Man dwelling with his fellowmen
Would honor on himself confer;
Alone with Nature — only then
Is he an honest worshiper.

MY HARP.

While wand'ring about in the meadow one morning,
A harp, long neglected, by chance there I found;
Attuned were its strings, which awoke without warning,
And lo, from them came a sweet musical sound!
Enchanted I listened, the music increasing,
And oh, what a joy to my heart it still brings,
As ever rich melody flows without ceasing,
As wander soft winds o'er its magical strings.

A lark, mounting high in the blue sky, was singing
In rythmical measures, clear, fervent and strong.
The notes from its beak, while it upward was winging,
Flowed back in a beautiful ripple of song.
The cords of the harp were in tune with the wild bird,
And throbbed 'neath the weight of a melody pure;
No song to my heart like the music I then heard—
In mem'ry 'twill live while my life shall endure.

That beautiful morn, oh, I ne'er shall forget it,
The meadow with cowslips and violets sweet;
The clear, silver brook winding peacefully through it,
The song-bird which rose from the grass 'neath my feet.
The bird in the picture is evermore singing;
I feel the sweet breath of that June morning blown,
And hear the rich notes of that melody ringing,
And know that the harp which I found was my own.

MUSIC.

At early morn a happy, laughing child,
With notes of mirth, filled all the air with song,
Which rang out with a freedom, careless—wild,
As Summer hours passed merrily along.
All, all was mirth; no notes of sympathy
As from a heart deep-stirred for others' woe
Was heard. Without this strain of melody
The music was morn's blush to day-god's glow—
As slowly opening bud to flower full-blown,
As tiny shrub to acorn-tree full grown.

The hours flew on; a cloud shut out the sun—
A cloud of sorrow, charged with bitter pain;
A minor strain awoke, thenceforth to run,
As sighing winds and softly murmuring rain,
Or, song-notes dipped in waves of human tears,
Flowing from heart all bruised and bleeding—torn
By thorns which line the path of later years,
And weight of sorrows grievous to be borne.
And there was music then; each note of song
Trembled with weight of melody so sweet
That all who listened would the strain prolong,
And wished the singer the sweet song repeat.

WINTER IN NEW ENGLAND.

Cold blows the wind—a chilling blast;
Dull, ashen clouds the sky o'ercast;
From North to South, from East to West,
From Morn 'til Night,
The storm-king weaves o'er Nature's breast
A robe of white.

From out the dark and stormy cloud,
Old Boreas blows the whitening shroud;
In trumpet blasts, sharp, fierce, and loud,
He rules the hour;
Cold, cruel, heartless, seeming proud
To show his pow'r.

WINTER IN NEW ENGLAND.

The "Bees of Winter," day and night,
Swarm through the air in wild delight;
A pleasing, aye! enchanting sight,
In coming down,
The vales to robe in spotless white—
The hills to crown.

The laughter of the flowing rills
No more the air with music fills;
The grinding of the water-mills
No more is heard,
And hushed are all the merry trills
Of woodland bird.

The streams and lakes, from shore to shore,
Are spanned by seamless bridges o'er,
Polished and smooth as marble floor,
O'er which we glide
On bars of steel, above the roar
Of muffled tide.

Soft parian wreaths festoon the trees
With decorations all to please,
'Til, shaken by the passing breeze,
Or kissed by sun,
They join the streamlets, by degrees
Their course to run.

A silence in the forest lies
And filleth all the sombre skies;
A universal death denies
All, save a tomb,
To every fond, sweet, glad surprise
Of woodland bloom.

But deep beneath the cloak of snow,
Down in their silent beds below,
The flowers are sleeping, and we know
That from this tomb
They soon will spring with freshened glow
Of life and bloom.

ELUSIVE SONG.

At morn, at noon, at twilight tide,
All times and everywhere,
Echoes of song about me glide
On the delusive air.

And now and then a note or two
Falls clearly on my ear,
Then dies away in ether blue,
And is no longer here.

I try to catch the merry notes,
But trembling, as with fear,
A silence falls on fairy throats
Whenever I draw near.

While lying 'neath the apple tree,
In half awakened dream,
I hear the sweetest melody
Floating on sunlight's beam.

NEW-YEAR'S MORNING.

The purpling footsteps of the morn
Now in the East appear,
And herald that again is born
Another glad New Year!

That, in the land beyond the sea,
The gods in power awoke,
And from the vast eternity
Another year bespoke!

And will Time never, never cease?
Will evening follow morn?
As fast as one shall find release,
Another one be born?

Will we poor midges of an hour—
Mere moths about the flame—
Clothed with a little transient power,
Exist but in a name?

A MOUNTAIN PICTURE.

I've a picture and a poem
Ever present in my mind,
It has beauty and enchantment
Only known unto its kind;
'Tis a picture in the mountains,
When the balmy breath of June,
'Mid the lofty pines and cedars,
Plays for all a magic tune.

A blue lake, calm and placid,
Typifying perfect rest,
As it cradles in its bosom
The tall mountain's snowy crest;
From its mirror is reflected,
Unto each observant eye,
Every cloud and bird that passes
O'er the bosom of the sky.

When the early twilight shadows
    Fall upon this mountain lake,
And the sportive trout, in leaping,
    Ripples on its bosom make,
Then I see an angler gently
    Push out slowly from the shore,
And go whipping of the waters
    Where the shadows fold them o'er.

Now a trout has struck the bright lure,
    And the lithe rod swerves and bends,
And the reel is singing sweetly
    As the line its freedom lends—
And the angler, all expectant,
    Plays the "beauty" with a skill
Which foreshadows that the ending
    Will mark well a splendid "kill."

Thus the picture ever haunts me,
    With a beauty which, for aye,
Holds enchained my brightest fancy
    By the hours of night and day,
And I wish that life forever
    Could be blessed with such a boon,
Where the trout are ever "striking"
    And the time is always June.

THE SNOW-PLANT OF THE SIERRAS.

Thou ruddy stranger, who may know
Why thou shouldst bloom midst ice and snow?
Ice proves to bloom a deadly foe,
        Is often said,
But here thou bloomest with a glow
        Of flaming red!

Lone, frigid flower of frost and storm,
'Round which the "bees of winter" swarm,
Thou seemest ever bright and warm
        Unto the eye;
Yet cold as ice is thy red form,
        Thou blooming lie!

WHAT IS POETRY?

You ask me what is poetry?
'Tis evening wind's soft tone
Returning from the deep blue sea,
Where all day it hath blown.

The crimson blush of fleecy cloud
At kiss of morning light;
Soft evening shades when first the shroud
Falls from the hand of Night.

The gushing of the mountain rill,
The soft wind's whisperings
To forests wild, when all is still
Save their faint echoings.

The murmur of the deep sea waves
Complaining to the shore;
The wave of grasses o'er the graves
Of those who are no more.

'Tis the bright crimson of the skies
Melting to purple hue,
When daylight softly fades and dies
As darkness shades the blue.

It is the rose without the thorn,
The joy without the pain;
The pleasant, peaceful Summer morn
After the chilling rain.

The song-bird calling to its mate
In forest, deep and wild;
All beauties which the soul elate—
The laugh of merry child.

The loving smile and tender tone,
The glance of woman's eye,
Are truest poems ever known
Beneath the starry sky.

EVENING.

Silence reigns supreme about us,
And the evening shadows creep
Up from hill-environed valley,
Where they rally,
To enshroud the rugged steep,
And to hush the woodland music,
Lulling all the birds to sleep.

Off to westward, mark the glamour!
Pink and saffron all the sky;
Hear, the gorgeous day in dying,
Softly sighing,
As the low winds flutter by,
Coming slowly in from seaward,
In the valleys here to lie.

Watch the shadows as they deepen
'Round about the nearer hills;
Mark the brooklet's low-voiced singing,
And the winging
Of the graceful whippoorwills,
As they flit like restless spirits
O'er the meadows and the rills.

See! the shining lamps of heaven
Pierce the gloom with golden ray,
And the silv'ry moonbeams streaming
O'er us gleaming,
Chases all the gloom away,
Rendering the night more pleasant
Than the dazzling hours of day.

Hear the chirping of the crickets;
See the fire-fly's fitful glow;
Now the gentle dew is falling,
And the calling
Of the katydids below
Comes from out the golden willows,
Swaying gently to and fro.

Stretched upon the ferns and mosses,
Sweet it is at ease to rest;
Night resistless is in wooing
And the cooing
Of her Naiads' sweet request
Is o'erpowering, and we slumber,
By their witching presence blest.

THE RAIN.

A sudden silence fills the air,
And then a low-voiced breeze,
Soft-wingéd, steals across the moor
And murmurs through the trees.
To sheltering groves the song birds flee
At boom of heaven's artillery.

The dark clouds from the Western sky
In unison advance.
The storm-king draws his glittering sword—
A brilliant, flashing lance;
His breath sweeps o'er the wood and plain—
A veritable hurricane.

The sturdy oak sways 'neath the blast,
The lake is lashed to foam,
And, in a wild, fierce jubilee,
Now rules the raging storm,
While o'er the woods and verdant plain
There falls o'er all the welcome rain.

TO THE SPORTSMEN OF THE HILLS.

I.

Ye lovers of the pine-clad hills and lakes,
Which mirror every line of heaven's face;
Who through the tangled copse of mountains trace
The royal game, whose magic presence makes
Your being tremble with a sweet desire
To win the prize—grand trophy of the chase—
The antlered stag, with eyes a-lit with fire;
Noblest of game beneath the rolling sun!
Perfection's grace, beyond comparison;
Proud as old Lucifer, a lord of kings,
His movements seeming less of feet than wings.
What grander theme for my poor pen than he?
Of sportsmen's paradise the deity.

Yet not of him alone I fain would speak;
Naught that exists but in itself is weak;
Of things we love, one-half or more is lent
From all things forming their environment.
The violet we love not half so well
Elsewhere than in its mossy, fern-clad dell,
Where dews bejewel every leaf and thorn,
When golden sunbeams paint the scene at morn.
The lily—blowing from her scented horn
The incense of the gods—to beauty born,
Acknowledged queen of all the floral field,
Her throne must sit, or else the scepter yield.
Each one must on all other things depend,
Or, all would be but one—beginning, end.
Nature this law of recompense confers;
No king could be, without his worshipers.

Some are content to learn from others' books,
    But with such wisdom comes the master's ills;
The sportsman gleans his lessons from the brooks,
    And from the everlasting green-clad hills.
Nature of all things is the primal source;
    Go to her fountain-head and wisdom learn.
A torpid liver, if not something worse,
    Affects most minds that from her pages turn.

He is a free man who himself sets free;
The basest slaves of all boast liberty,
Yet never have on earth their souls been stirred
By e'en the faintest meaning of that word.
For liberty and light and truth are one—
The grandest trinity beneath the sun;
And he more near is free from base alloy
Who can the most of these the most enjoy.

Pure liberty of action and of thought
Are priceless gems, and ne'er too dearly bought;
The hills, the plains, the lakes, the mountains high,
Are Nature's stores in which these treasures lie.
Would you possess these matchless jewels rare?
Then mount your steed and to the hills repair.
Hark, to the horn! for now its cheering note
Upon the morning air in quavers float.

II.

Ho! for the chase, for the royal chase,
    With the music of horns and hounds;
On a noble steed to take the lead
    Of them all on the hunting grounds;
To feel the blood, a rushing flood,
    Go bounding, leaping through the veins,
And know the field we need not yield
    While we keep our grip on the reins.

Urging our steed to his utmost speed,
    We sail like a bird on the wing,
While the very wind is left behind,
    Heavy-wingéd with sounds that ring
Up from the dells, like legions of bells,
    Swelling over the valleys and hills;
The echoes rebound with a double sound,
    Then fade into musical trills.

Hard on the pack we follow the track
    Of the wild game speeding away;
Our noble steed increasing his speed
    At each touch of the spur or flay,
'Till we see the prize before our eyes,
    For, behold, it is brought to bay,
And now before us panting lies—
    We've won, huray! huray!! huray!!!

RETROSPECTION.

When weary and worn with the rowing
    Against the swift current of Time,
Whose billows in anger are showing
    Their tiger-like spirit of crime—
In deep, sullen growls all about me
    Are leaping with snarls upon deck,
And glaring in fierceness they mock me,
    And claim my frail craft for a wreck.
Yet, 'spite of it all, I am fearless,
    Though catching no gleam from the shore;
About me all threatening and cheerless—
    I love to cease pulling the oar.

To drift idly backward and leeward;
    To lie again calmly at rest,
Where youth's favored winds blowing seaward
    Awoke fondest hopes in my breast;
Again through the woodlands and lea-lands
    To wander in peace all alone,
Or, down on the bright golden sea-sands,
    To list to the wild billows moan;
To lie in the meadows and smother
    Regrets, with the clover blooms sweet,
Where often in youth, with another,
Love rendered our wand'rings complete.

There again to watch the kine nipping
    The grasses bejeweled with dew,
The barn-swallows gracefully dipping
    In the waves where the pond-lilies grew;
To steal o'er the lawn 'neath the arches,
    Where clambered the sweet blooming vine,
With footsteps to zephyr-played marches,
    While drinking of memory's wine.
If years, with their burden of sorrows,
    Do naught but endear the fond past,
How sweet will be all of the morrows
    With old scenes preserved 'till the last?

How painfully sweet to my vision
    Are all the loved scenes of my youth;
I knew them when every decision
    Was founded alone upon truth;
Before the foul dust of long travel
    Had grimed its way into my soul;
Before the rough stones and hard gravel
    I'd trod, on the way to the goal.
I love my youth's innocent viewing,
    Forgetting the pain and the tears,
Which followed my young life's undoing—
    The rape of my innocent years.

NEW-YEAR REFLECTIONS.

One year older, one year more
    Added to those past and gone;
Climbing toward the second score,
    What a weight bears every one!
Time engulfs the joy and tear,
    Plucks the thistle and the rose;
Knows no pity—knows no fear—
    As it ever onward flows.

Every morn, however bright,
    Is but fleeting as the wave—
Flashes of a passing light,
    Guiding travelers to the grave.
Every step wherever trod,
    Every pulse and every breath,
Nears our home beneath the sod—
    Urn of universal death.

Mem'ry holds but pleasures few,
    Sorrows with us long remain;
Joys fade like the morning dew,
    Griefs engender lingering pain.
Thus, through shifting of the years,
    Heap the burdens of distress;
Fall more freely, Sorrow's tears,
    Heavier grows our loneliness.

" I am dying," spake the year,
    Dim, uncertain was his sight;
Trembled oft the saddened tear,
    As approached his final night.
" I have sorrowed, I have joyed,
    I have felt my bosom glow
With a warmth no fear alloyed;
    But now drifts alone the snow."

Curtained grows his failing eye,
    Faint and fainter comes his breath;
Moans his last despairing sigh,
    Now the Old Year meets his death.
Breaks the morning bright and clear,
    Fresh and joyous, clear and bright—
Time appears all hearts to cheer,
    With the blessings of delight.

May it be that for us all,
    When our year of life shall close—
We shall step out from the pall
    Bright as New Year's morning rose;
This life prove a training school,
    Where the heart and head are taught
Noble actions, and the rule
    Learn'd that leads to higher thought.

THE DEATH OF SUMMER.

Heard ye that sigh
Go by?
It seemed to travel toward the sky.
    Methought it said:
  "Lo, she is dead;
    The power of Summer's life has fled;
Dimmed is the lustre of her eye."

Her lovely days
And ways
Die mid yonder sunset haze;
    Unto the sight
    Her tender light
    Fading in folds of Autumn night,
A peaceful beauty rare displays.

The East was bright
With light
And in the West retreating night;
    To me they said:
  "Weep for the dead,
    The Autumn with the earth is wed,
Look and behold, we speak aright."

And it was true,
There blew
More chilling winds than Summer knew;
To her their breath
Was instant death;
To me their mournful voices saith:
"Her spirit fades with yonder blue."

The roses sigh
And die;
Their leaves all torn and withered lie
Upon the ground;
A solemn sound
Fills all the airy space around—
A sobbing, wierd, heart-touching cry.

The lilies pray
To-day:
"Oh, let us here no longer stay;
With Summer's sun
Our work is done,
Our race of life is fully run,
Oh, bear us to our tomb away."

The woodland choir
Retire,
To sing no more is their desire;
No cherry note
From feathered throat
Upon the balmy air will float
'Till Summer's smile shall it inspire.

Some morn divine,
With mine,
I trust her spirit may entwine
And live for aye,
Where lustrous day
Shall chase all thoughts of gloom away;
Where comes of death no warning sigh.

THE PROPOSAL.

October, dear hazy old fellow,
    I love your sun's golden beams,
As over the forest and meadow
    His mellow light lazily streams,
Throwing over the mountains a mantle
    So mystic, so subtle and fine
That it adds a new charm to all Nature,
    And robes it in beauty divine.

You bring to my mind many treasures
    From memory's hallowéd store;
They are dear, yet a tinge of your sadness
    Makes them dearer a thousand times more;
For your soft breezes seem almost human,
    As they echo the sigh of my heart,
That the dearest, best love of the human
    Is formed here on earth but to part.

I thank thee, dear old October,
    For reviving those scenes of the past;
They are part of my soul's dearest treasures,
    And forever and ever shall last.
The waters of Leathe shall not o'er them
    The waves of oblivion cast;
They shall dwell fresh and green in my mem'ry,
    Forever present, yet past.

October, can you keep a secret?
    Will you keep it and not tell the breeze?
For he's such a fun-loving fellow
    He'd surely be telling the trees,
And the leaves would be sure to o'erhear it
    And down to the meadows they'd go,
And soon the meadows would be telling
    Their beautiful mantle of snow.

And the snowflake as it mounts on the sunbeam
  To its home far away in the cloud
Would soon be telling the thunder,
  And the thunder would echo it loud;
And the lightning would surely be listening,
  And thus my secret would steal,
And one flash of his dazzling brightness
  Would all of my secret reveal.

So, you'll keep it, won't you, October?
  I know you'll be true to the trust,
And tell only her, October,
  Tell her only you must,
For I know she loves you, October,
  For your loveliness, not for your name,
And for this you may tell her, October,
  I wish you and I were the same.

There now, go tell her my secret,
  Tell her 'tis not fancy but real,
And what I have spoken is only
  A very small part that I feel.
Do you pray, dear October? then let us kneel,
  And of our heavenly Father request,
That, whatever her answer may be,
  That she may richly be blest.

NOVEMBER.

Robed in sackcloth and in ashes,
  Is the form of Nature now;
Her eye no more with gladness flashes—
  Sorrow sits upon her brow.

Mournful, weary, heavy-hearted;
  She fills the air with tender sighs—
  Fills all the air with tears and sighs—
Summer's glory is departed,
  With yonder azure sunset dies.

Deep gloom and sadness covers all,
  The fields and flowers are crisp and sear;
The forest leaves now fade and fall,
  While feeble grows the dying year.

TO THE MOURNING DOVE.

What renders thee so desolate?
    Why these sad notes, so soft and low?
Has cruel, unrelenting fate
    Decreed it shall be ever so;
        Through light and shade
        Thy song be made
Of notes that only speak of woe?

Why this refrain, this sad lament?
    Art thou too weighted down with sin,
And hast become a penitent,
    Hoping some heaven to enter in?
        By price of tears
        Called out by fears
Hope thou God's favor, too, to win?

By what arch sin from their first state
    Was thy race from their Eden hurled,
And doomed to roam disconsolate
    O'er this death-stricken, dreary world?
        Doth thy sweet breast
        Hope for a rest
    Where Summer skies are e'er unfurled?

A world wherein no notes of woe
Are ever heard, but music sweet
As chime of bells or brooklet's flow
Doth ears enchanted ever greet?
Loved bird below,
Beyond the flow
Of death's dark stream, I trust, we'll meet.

THE BURIAL OF SUMMER.

Autumn has come with its funeral train,
Bearing the corpse of sweet Summer along,
While the mourning clouds great tear-drops rain,
And the winds are piping a mournful song.

The King from the Northland sent out his hosts,
Lovely Summer to conquer and slay;
Silent they came as an army of ghosts,
Traveling only by night all the way.

As Summer lay sleeping, they poisoned her breath
With the crystaline poisons they bear;
Then clammy and cold lay sweet Summer in death,
Terror-chilled was the grief-stricken air.

The roses for love of her smiles quickly died,
The fair lilies in grief bowed their heads;
The velvety grasses are withered and dried
Where the life-chilling breath o'er them spreads.

Alas! alas! that sweet Summer should die.
That her warm, rosy lips should grow cold,
That curtained should be her bright, beaming eye,
Her rich garments be flecked with the mold.

That all her bright smiles should fade in a day,
Her sweet story of love be untold,—
Her laughter should die in sobbings away
With the damp chilling winds of the wold.

AMID GOD'S GREATER THOUGHTS.

I stood upon the mountain's crest,
And looked across the vales,
And saw the rivers rushing down
Their steep and winding trails,

Foaming and leaping from the peaks,
All covered o'er with snow;
Kissed by the warmth of Summer's breath
Into a crystal flow.

Some placid lakes like silver shone,
Beneath the evening sun,
And some were like to flaming fire;
A beauty, every one!

The verdured valleys far below,
Were wrapped in gloaming deeps,
Though sunshine gilded all the spires,
And bathed in light the steeps.

And thus, thought I, it is in life,
For all who truth would know;
All, all must climb from out the depths—
The shadows lie below!

Climb up the steep and rocky way,
Climb on and up, and learn,
From these grand, towering thoughts of God,
All littleness to spurn.

TOMB OF HELEN HUNT JACKSON.

Our daughter who stood on the brow of Parnassus,
    And flung to the world her bright jewels of song,
Hath lain down her harp, and no more will enchant us,
    With the notes of her music so fervent and strong;
No more will the scent of her heart's ardent roses,
    Be thrown on the mountain air, careless and wild,
For here on its bosom now sweetly reposes
    All that was earthly of fair Nature's sweet child.

Each peak in the range of these lofty mountains,
    Each wild rocky glen, and each cataract's tone;
Each silvery spray of these wild dashing fountains,
    She loved, and their spirit made part of her own.
She wooed as a lover the voices of Nature,
    And drew from her bosom the thoughts of her soul,
Caressing in fondness each wild mountain feature,
    Caught all the bright gleamings which over them roll.

Rest well, gentle spirit, the tones of thy mother
    Soft lullabies singing are heard for thee now;
The brooklet—thy sister, the mountain—thy brother,
    Are weaving bright chaplets to cover thy brow.
Rest well, while the winds softly breathe o'er thy pillow
    Æolian strains 'mid the boughs of the pines,
While down by the streamlet the bright golden willow,
    In sorrow, its gentle form sweetly inclines.

II.

'Tis fitting that she calmly lie
    On this enchanted spot,
Where stranger's footsteps passing by,
    Its peace disturbeth not;
Where morning sun shall sweetly shine
Through clustering boughs of waving pine,
    By none on earth forgot,
For she, a mountain flower, whose bloom
Still sweetly lingers 'round her tomb.

'Tis sweet indeed to visit her,
    As here in peace she lies,
Alone in her wild sepulcher
    Beneath the mountain skies;
To place a fragment of God's thought
Upon her tomb; 'twas these that taught
    Her noble mind to rise
Above the clouds and storms of earth,
To regions of a purer birth.

Breathe softly winds, breathe faint and low,
    Over the mountain's brow;
By moon's pale rays, by day-god's glow
    Attune thy accents now;
And morning winds, bring ye sweet chimes
And breath of prayer from other climes;
    For earth will not allow
A flower so pure to here decay,
And waste its sweetness all away.

This gate called death she did not fear,
    But deemed it just the way
That leads to loved ones grown more dear
    In fields of endless day;
But the to-morrow veiled from sight
By sombre shadows called to-night,
    Which fade at death away;
Beyond the tomb, could we but see,
God's love lights all eternity.

There in the fair light of His love
    Forever more to sing,
Where is no night, in realms above,
    Her soul is blossoming ;
Where every joy of mortal worth
Is blessed with an eternal birth,
    On wave of spirit wing,
Forever more to upward rise
And heaven find one glad surprise.

THE FONTAINE-QUI-BOUILLE.

Down from the mountains to the West
Springing from out their snow-capped crest
A merry dashing streamlet flows,
Which in the sunlight sparkling glows
From morn 'till eve, from eve 'till dawn,
As gleefully it murmurs on,
In tones of joy which never cease,
As o'er each rocky precipice
It leaps and laughs the hours away,
From Spring 'til Winter's chilling day.

Along this streamlet's winding bed,
Grandeur and Beauty firmly wed,
Present to the observing eye,
Unequaled charms beneath the sky.
On either side the mountains rise
Until they seem to reach the skies;
No grander path on earth than this
Which leads to their metropolis—
A mountain on whose hoary head
Stern Winter ever makes his bed,
And breathes upon the world below
His cooling breath from drifts of snow.

THE FONTAINE-QUI-BOUILLE.

No pen can write, no tongue can tell,
The beauties of a mountain dell;
The magic glories which there lie,
All power of speech or brush defy,
For Nature's voices in each tone
Reveal a beauty all her own;
And man can only faintly feel
Her best thoughts through his bosom steal,
When her sweet, subtile power to bless,
Is felt alone in quietness,
Which at a word do take alarm,
And lose their best and truest charm.

If you would know her sweetest mood,
Woo her alone in solitude,
Where by the ear no sound is heard
Save rustling leaf by soft wind stirred,
Or thrilling notes of some wild bird,
Whose merry song, in harmony
With liquid voice of mountain stream,
Echoes along from rock to tree,
So softly that they ever seem,
A memory of some faint dream.

Such spots are found each Summer day,
Along the Fontaine-qui-bouille,
Which throws aloft its silver spray
As, o'er the granite boulders dashing,
It gambols on so light and free,
In merry mood its waters splashing,
In tones of purest melody;
While the great mountains ever throw
Their shadows o'er the path below,
Which winds along the pleasant stream,
To spots more fair than poet's dream:
Their perfect beauty never marred,
Where Heloise and Abelard,
Or kindred spirits, such as they,
Might pass the sultry days away.

There velvet grasses, pure and sweet,
Fit carpets weave for angels' feet;
Where blooms the wild, red passion rose,
Which o'er the granite boulders creeping,
Gives unto every wind that blows
Rich odors, which their onward sweeping
Carries to each, to one and all,
Whose pathways through these mountains fall.
Amid these scenes the air is rife
With ruddy health — the rose of life;
That gift supreme, and all divine,
Which thrills the heart like sparkling wine;
By which to mortals here is given
The power to taste the joys of heaven.

CHEYENNE CAÑON.

Along thy dim-lit aisles I tread,
And listen to the songs e'er sung,
By crystal waters, which here thread
Their way, thy cast-off crowns among;
Strange thoughts unspoken o'er me steal,
And to myself, myself reveal.

Who am I? What is this I see?
An inner world I ne'er have known?
The soul of some sweet mystery,
Comes o'er me here with thee alone;
A voiceless spirit wings the glen —
Soul of the mountain of Cheyenne!

Here Nature's silent voices speak;
Would all their melody might feel!
Like notes from spirit songster's beak,
Music of feeling they reveal.
All words are harsh and meaningless
Compared with Nature's power to bless.

Here, in thy shadows, soft winds creep,
And tall pines pierce the mellow sky;
The golden-fingered willows weep,
And silver streamlets murmur by!
A hush falls on the lips of men
Within thy aisles, oh! grand Cheyenne!

THE MOUNTAIN BROOK.

From the fountain,
In the mountain,
Rushing ever to the sea,
Always, ever,
And forever,
Voicing purest melody.
Glancing, dancing, foaming, prancing,
To a music all its own;
With a motion as entrancing
As its magic mellow tone.

Night enshrouded,
Day beclouded,
Silvered with the moonlight's gleam;
In the twilight,
'Neath the starlight,
Or the sunlight's golden beam;
Nothing evermore can calm its
Ceaseless efforts to unfold,
The pure spirit speaking from its
White-lipped waters, sweet and cold.

THE MAID TO THE OCEAN.

Roll gently, ye billows,
Ye deep rolling billows —
Roll gently, roll gently, I pray,
As light swaying willows,
As sad, weeping willows;
In soft breeze of bright Summer day.

For over the ocean,
The deep, restless ocean,
There saileth a ship for this shore:
Be gentle thy motion,
Create no commotion
'Til its voyage safely be o'er.

I now ask it, oh, sea,
Oh, thou deep, heaving sea,
For that ship bears my lover true;
Bring him safely to me
And forever will we
Be grateful and thankful to you.

THE OLD SEA CAVE.

I wandered to-day to the old sea cave,
Where often my love and I
Have gazed with delight on the breaking wave,
As it dashed its foam on high;
As it shouted aloud an anthem grand,
In tones that were deep and strong;
It said to each heart in the wide, wide world:
"Let your love be like my song."

Then our hearts were light and our faith was strong,
In our love so sweet and true;
We said it should be like the ocean's song,
Forever the same, yet new;
We said it should be like the ocean wide,
And the rocks upon the shore,
I the world to her, she to me a bride,
Forever and evermore.

But the storms came on and the billows rolled
Through the cave down by the sea;
As the waves beat fierce and the winds blew cold,
They swept my love from me.
Oh, my sweet love, and my dear, dear love,
So lost in the raging storm,
Come back to my heart from the sky above,
With thy love so true and warm.

Come back, come back, to the old sea cave,
And list to the billows roar;
Come back to my heart as the ocean wave
Comes back to the waiting shore.
Then a soul-voice said to my anguished soul,
'Twas my love of long ago:
"My heart shall be thine while the sea waves roll,
Aye! after they cease to flow."

THE BIRTH OF DAY.

The lake! the lake, the mountain lake, invitingly now lies,
A liquid gem of beauty rare, beneath the Summer skies.
The wind's low winging fans my cheek and whispers—"Come away
To scenes amid the mountains, where first falls the light of day."

There, where the skies the mountains kiss, are pleasures without pain;
And tangled through the leaves and grass, the Sun-sprite's golden skein;
And when the gloaming shadows fall, at holy hour of eve,
The merry Wood-nymphs, through them all, the silvery moonbeams weave.

When morning breaks—did'st ever see the morning's face at birth,
Where cloudless skies are linked about the giants of the earth?
The blush—aye, fairer than the rose the infant there appears,
While his fair brow fond mother Night baptizes with her tears.

The sun comes on—the infant Morn arises on its wings,
And to each gulch and valley deep a robe of beauty flings;
The tears night gave at parting there are turned to jewels now,
And flash resplendent—royal gems studding a royal brow.

The crystal streams now laugh and leap, babbling with merry glee;
All life bounds up with joyous step, from slumber's fetters free;
Morn, now full-fledged in blue and gold, mounts up the shining way,
As Night, the chrysalis, unfolds the butterfly of Day.

UNIV. OF
CALIFORNIA

OCEAN COURSERS

OCEAN COURSERS.

Down by the sea where the strong coursers thunder,
As galloping on they come in with the tide;
Snorting and shaking their white manes in wonder,
That freedom to them by the shore is denied;
Charging and champing they hurl themselves boldly
'Gainst the gray rocks, or leap over the sand,
Until weakened, exhausted, and shuddering coldly,
They bow with regret to the power of the land.

Back to the great deep they creep with emotion,
Nursing their anger aroused by defeat;
May God help the ship which, out in mid-ocean,
These wild, angry coursers should happen to meet;
For there they may rise where their power is unbroken,
And rule with destruction again and again;
How many grand vessels have gone down unspoken
By aught that returned to the knowledge of men!

Far from all aid, at these wild coursers' mercy,
Tossed like a shell by the force of their will;
Trembling a moment, and then in the blue sea,
The vessel goes down, and forever is still.
On sweep the coursers still leaping and calling
For vengeance 'gainst all who would rule o'er the wave;
Their voice, when in anger, the bravest appalling
At thought that defeat means a watery grave.

BEAUTIFUL MEADOWS.

Beautiful meadows, down by the river,
Dotted with daisies and buttercups sweet;
Jeweled with dewdrops which sparkle and quiver
When night, before morning, beats hasty retreat.
Beautiful meadows, beautiful night;
Beautiful, beautiful morning light.

WHEN ROVER DIED.

When Rover died, our childish hearts were filled
With a wilder grief than we yet had known.
Our tears fell fast; we had not yet been skilled
To sorrow hide; the fallow ground unsown
Of that distrust which harvests but deceit;
No tares yet grew amid the tender wheat.
For honest grief we sobbed and cried,
When Rover died.

When Rover died, the pleasant Spring-time sun
Shed o'er the hills its wealth of virgin gold;
But sorrow palled our hearts, and every one
Was truly sad; a friend had left the fold—
A friend for love of whom our every heart
Was wrung with pain, at thought that we should part.
Our bosoms heaved with sorrow's tide,
When Rover died.

Calmly he lay upon the grassy lawn,
Silent, as if but sleeping out his night;
We wondered that he woke not with the dawn,
We could not reconcile death with the sight
Of our loved playmate lying there so still;
We hoped he would awake, we said, "He will."
And thus for comfort vainly tried,
When Rover died.

We buried him down by the garden wall,
At sunset's hour; out from the cooling shade
The whip-poor-will sent forth its mournful call
As if the cadence of its notes were made
To harmonize with hearts that mourned, while night,
With kindly hand, veiled from our sight
The scene, the sense of peace denied,
When Rover died.

THE MOUNTAIN STREAM.

The gods to thee, oh, mountain stream,
  No thought of beauty have denied;
Fairer thou art than angels' dream,
  As ever on thy waters glide.
Thy every motion is of grace;
  Thy voicing music's perfect tone;
Fair is the beauty of thy face,
  As fair as Beauty's very own.

I bound to greet thee, oh, my love!
  Oh, love of mine, so sweet and fair,
Within thy home, in glen and grove,
  Where incense ladens all the air!
Maid of the hills and mountains grand,
  Pearl of the land from sea to sea;
Thy charms the love of all command —
  Thy pure, unsoiled virginity!

When worn and weary with the strife,
  That fills the city's busy mart —
That withers all the flowers of life,
  And renders sore and tired the heart,
I turn to thee for rest and peace,
  Oh, fount of joy and perfect bliss;
In thee I find from care release —
  Sweet comfort in thy cooling kiss.

Emblem of purity and truth,
  Healer of sorrow and of pain,
With thee I find the joys of youth
  Revived and living now again!
Thy joys far sweeter now appear
  Than vista of expectancy —
Though radiant, it is less dear
  Than that of thy sweet memory.

PLEASURES A-FIELD.

When the whistle of the quail
  Trembles on the quiet air,
Buckle on your shooting mail,
  To the open fields repair!
      It is pleasure
      Without measure
      Thus in leisure
  Without care
On the hillside, in the stubble,
To shake off all earthly trouble,
  And all foes of peace to dare.
There is nothing for the liver
  Half so good — it cannot fail
To arouse it — bless the giver
  Of the sport of shooting quail.

MY CIGAR.

The fragrant smoke from my cigar
Curls up in wreaths of blue;
Idly my thoughts drift now afar
From old scenes to the new.
My youthful hours I live again,
Old visions come to me;
Freedom from care without a pain
Is drawn from memory.

CHORUS:–There is no hour so sweet to me
As when I live afar
In those loved days of memory,
While smoking my cigar.

It serves to sooth the cares of life,
And banish every pain;
It lulls to ease all thoughts of strife
And warms life's chilling rain.
No aid so potent now to me,
No friend so good and true;
Would that all hearts could float as free
As its light waves of blue.

CHORUS:–There is no hour so sweet to me
As when I live afar
In those loved days of memory,
While smoking my cigar.

I envy not the lord his wealth,
Though poverty my lot;
No blessing adds to ruddy health
When troubles are forgot.
True magic balm for every heart—
Wooer of visions fair—
Before thy charms cares all depart,
And dwell not anywhere.

CHORUS:–There is no hour so sweet to me
As when I live afar
In those loved days of memory,
While smoking my cigar.

WHEN THE JACK-SNIPE COMES.

When the Jack-snipe comes,
We will be
Off to meet him in the marshes
By the sea;
There amid the reeds and rushes,
Which our every footstep crushes,
While the murky water gushes
To our knee,
We will be,
When
the
Jack-
snipe
comes.

When the warm rains come
In the Spring,
And the migratory birds are
On the wing;
Then of pleasures there are none,
Like to those with dog and gun,
Where the sluggish waters run,
To the sea,
Dreamily,
When
the
Jack-
snipe
comes.

What sport we will have
By and by,
When the sombre shades are drifting
O'er the sky;
In the falling of the year,
When the leaves are brown and sear,
Then the sport we love so dear
We will try,
By and by,
When
the
Jack-
snipe
comes.

When the leaves turn brown,
    Mark the day;
To the marshes and the meadows
    We'll away;
When the mallards southward fly,
And the lilies droop and die,
With the Summer's farewell sigh
    We will say,
    Bless the day,
When
    the
        Jack-
            snipe
                comes.

"Scaipe, scaipe!" hear the note
    Of the game;
Ever thus from marsh and meadows
    Just the same.
See him twisting in his flight,
To the sportsman what a sight!
Filling with a strange delight
    All his frame,
    Else he's tame,
When
    the
        Jack-
            snipe
                comes.

TO THE OCEAN.

Oh! ocean deep,
Why dost thou weep?
And mourn and sob and never sleep?
  Is there no rest
  For thy poor breast,
  Unanswered still thy heart's request?
Must Sorrow's shades e'er o'er thee creep?

THE DRYAD'S CHAMBER.

I know a magic chamber where
The Queen of all the fairies dwells,
Within the mountains where the air
Is perfumed by the asphodels.
Where blue-bells ring their sweetest chimes,
At morn, at noon, at twilight dim ;
Where the arbutus clings and climbs,
And waters voice a constant hymn.

The wild rose clambers o'er its walls,
The ivy wraps its columns rouud,
Adorning all its stately halls
With grace that nowhere else is found.
The rocks moss-painted at the fount,
Are sprayed by filmy veils of mist,
Cooling this chamber as they mount
To cloud-land, by the sunbeams kissed.

Springing from out the rocky urns,
Set in the niches here and there,
Nodding and swaying are the ferns,
With every passing breath of air.
Depending from the ceiling green,
Are the deep-red laburnum bells,
And, shining brightly in between,
The dog-star pure its beauty tells.

All o'er its tessellated floor
Kind Nature weaves for it each Spring,
From entrance unto exit door,
A flower-bespangled carpeting.
There golden mango-apples grow,
And songbirds warble by the stream ;
The whole designed, I feel and know,
From Cupid's most enchanting dream !

And there the oriole is heard
Full oft to carol forth his lay ;
What minstrel sweeter than this bird,
Which Zephyr rocks the livelong day ?
A ball of gold across the shade
He seems, as here and there beheld,
Flitting athwart the dreamy glade,
And through the leafy emerald.

Oft there I love to ponder well,
The lessons from the hand divine ;
To catch the force of Beauty's spell,
And sip of Nature's richest wine.
Oh, Cupid ! Cupid ! would that I
Might ever dream such dreams of bliss,
For heaven must be very nigh
To such enchanting spots as this.

CATHEDRAL SPIRES — YOSEMITE.

No foot has pressed those stairways dizzy,
No hand has touched those silent bells;
No mortal sacristan there busy —
Silence alone the story tells.
Those aisles untrod, save by the spirits,
Whose mortal forms rest 'neath the sod;
They only have the power to hear its
Chimes of God.

SPRING.

She comes, she comes, the sweet, young bride,
In royal robes most rich and fair;
Her heralds, with a conscious pride,
With sweetest music fill the air.
The softest robes enfold her form,
The brightest jewels deck her brow;
Her smile destroys the Winter's storm,
And wreaths the land in beauty now.

Upon her cheeks the roses bloom,
And violets fill her tender eyes,
And on her evenings' early gloom,
The odor of sweet incense lies;
She smiles, and sighs, and laughs, and weeps
All in a day, her changing mood
With fleeting wing her bosom sweeps,
And thoughts of peace and rest exclude.

THE CALIFORNIA QUAIL.

The sportsmen of the Golden State
Pursue thee to a cruel fate,
From morning bright till evening late,
With trained canine,
They tramp thy haunts with thoughts elate
On thee to dine.

They hear thy whistling call, "Whee-we,"
Echoing oft, in accents free,
From mountain ranges to the sea,
As from thy throat
Issues thy hailing melody
In quavering note.

In vain thou seekest cover deep,
Thy hiding place thou canst not keep;
The very air thy odors steep,
And thus betray
Thy presence when thou wake or sleep,
By night or day.

The sportsman's dog with nostrils fine,
Scents out thy home and gives the sign,
And they together thus combine
To do thee ill;
But thou full oft escape design
Of scent and skill.

REFLECTIONS.

If men cared more for rod and gun,
For running streams and sparkling fountains,
For balmy breezes — golden sun,
Amid the valleys and the mountains,
They would be better and more free
From sordid care
And thoughts that wear
The lustre from nobility.

If men knew what true pleasures lie
Awaiting always for their coming,
Where mountains pierce the azure sky
And wild birds fill the air with humming,
They oft would drop the dross of trade,
And for a day
Throw care away,
And seek the wild woods' cooling shade.

If men cared less for power and gold,
Joy would remain, the heart grow lighter;
And pleasure walk with them when old;
The path of age be smooth and brighter.
Ashes of hope and wrecks of strife
Would less endure,
And leave secure,
The rule of Peace at close of life.

The fountain Ponce de Leon sought,
Is everywhere, and always flowing
With pleasures which cannot be bought,
But free to all the wise, who knowing
That life is naught, unless each hour
Some pleasures know,
And that the foe
To peace is greed of gold and power.

THE SEASONS.

Spring, the laughing and debonair
    Danseuse, with her many suits,
Plays a changing and sprightly air—
    Satin slippers and rubber boots!
Storm and sunshine follows her train;
    Laughter and tears she revels in—
Sobs as a maid for lover slain;
    Smiles as the maid who would one win.

Wreathed in a maze of golden curls,
    Bright she beams from the sunny South,
Lightly floating in merry whirls—
    Curves bewitching about her mouth!
Now she hides 'neath a "water-proof,"
    Storms and scolds like a termagant;
Plays sorry pranks with Trust and Truth—
    Leading coquet of all extant!

Trust and Truth with Summer confer,
    Coming down through a golden sky;
Bridle and reins of gossamer,
    Riding a gorgeous butterfly!
Filling the air with odors sweet,
    From flowery censers swinging free;
Lady-slippers encase her feet—
    Her song the soul of harmony.

Brushing the gold from off her wings
    Upon the hills and waving grain;
Blessing all with the gifts she flings
    Freely from off her magic train.
With languorous ease she flits along,
    Or rests in the shade of spreading tree,
Content to list to the drowsy song
    Of the buzzing fly or humble bee.

THE SEASONS.

Autumn comes with her brush and paints,
  Flecking the clouds with crimson hue;
Painting pictures fit for the saints,
  On the broad stretch of heaven's blue;
Changes the woods from green to brown,
  Colors the fruits a deeper red;
Gives the maples a golden crown —
  Form to color by her is wed.

She throws o'er all a mystic veil,
  Making the earth to truly seem
A record of some fairy tale,
  Or, some sweet thought of poet's dream.
She fills the air with tender sighs,
  And drapes the sun with filmy screen;
All flushed and tanned, at rest she lies,
  The sweetest sight the year hath seen.

Winter comes with his reindeers fleet,
  Over a robe of crystal snow;
Encased in furs from head to feet,
  While arctic winds most fiercely blow.
He kills the flowers, he binds the stream,
  He drives the birds in haste away;
He plucks the heat from sunlight's beam —
  A stern old king is Winter gray.

The great trees bend before the blast,
  And fling their bare arms to the sky;
A gloom o'er all the hills is cast,
  As he goes driving swiftly by.
But all within is bright and warm,
  While fireside stories speed the hours,
Where all secure from Winter's harm
  May bloom affection's sweetest flowers.

A SUMMER NOON.

Soft, mellow skies their arches fling
    Above us like a sea,
Where feathery cloudlets, slow of wing,
    Are floating dreamily.

A mystic veil of royal hue,
    The distant mountains hood,
And, like a robe of silvery blue,
    Lies on the lake and wood.

Deep silence broods o'er land and sea;
    Save meadow brook's soft tone,
And drowsy hum of honey-bee,
    No other sounds are known.

WITH MY OLD SHOT-GUN.

There may be pleasures greater, but I haven't found them out,
In this country where the game birds are a-flying all about,
Than to listen in the morning to the whistle of the quail,
As it echoes o'er the valley and from out the mountain vale;
Or to see the ducks a-winging o'er the fields and marshes wide,
Then alighting in the waters, o'er the waves to smoothly glide.
Then with buoyant expectations, with the rising of the sun,
I love to reap enjoyment
with
my
old
shot-
gun.

There's another always with me, trotting ever by my side;
To share my every pleasure is his constant care and pride;
With expressions of alertness, keen of scent and bright of eye,
It is seldom that a game bird undetected is passed by.
Now he's trailing up a "runner" that is dodging here and there,
See how cautiously he "works" him with a more than human care,
How it thrills my soul with pleasure, Lord! this is right royal fun,
To bag the gamy, toothsome quail
with
my
old
shot-
gun.

On the marshes in the morning, when at first the grayish light
Marks the hour when birds aquatic will begin their early flight;
With a silence all about me lying on the lea and lake,
As of breathless expectation waiting for the morn to wake;
I love to lie and listen for the whistle of the wings,
Which the "flappers" when low flying ever with their motion sings.
Then the pleasure is unmeasured when the sport is well begun,
And I drop the ducks about me
with
my
old
shot-
gun.

There's a wing-tipped, wily mallard seeking in the grass to hide,
Not another thus his equal will by no one be denied;
He would "fool the very devil," is of him a true report,
But this will not avail him now, he cannot fool Old Sport!
There he plunges in the water, diving low beneath the bank,
Pokes his head up where the lilies grow upon the water, rank,
But Old Sport goes plunging after and the bird his race has run;
Glorious sport this, in the Autumn,
with
my
old
shot-
gun.

A PRIMITIVE ANGLER.

Her face was a study for chisel or brush,
With skin indescribably white;
Underneath it the blood,
Like a pure crimson flood,
Spoke of health and enamored the sight.
Her fishing-cap sat on a cluster of curls,
Behind and before, just the same;
A "killing" cap 'twas,
And my heart took a pause,
For her beauty its strength overcame.

Her sweet, rosy lips and sea-shell-like ears,
Fine-fluted, transparent and thin,
Lent a charm to the sight,
And enhanced my delight
For the prize which I angled to win.
I sought by a glance, all too short to be rude,
To attract her attention to me;
But I found that this bait
Was not worth its own weight,
And no "catch" would it make, I could see.

I next tried a pose, but to this there arose
Not a smile or a flush to her face.
I arose, and then took
From my satchel a book;
I have known them all fears to displace.
The beauty sat silent for a half-hour or more,
While I was distracting my brain;
For could I find out
How to catch such a "trout!"
I never would angle again.

I next opened up my new book of bright flies,
And held them where she, too, could see;
In a moment I saw
That this card was a draw,
For she leaned sweetly over to me.
And as her soft breath fell warm on my cheek,
I felt I a good "strike" had made;
But I was not quite sure
That my line would endure
The "fight" with this beautiful maid.

I cleared up my throat with the thought to begin
And looked mildly up to her eyes;
But she never once took
Her glance from my book;
"More than trout are caught," thought I, "with flies."
We soon fell to talking of angling for trout;
The maid on one point was quite firm:
"Follow nature," she said,
"Success only is wed
To the hook which is hid in a worm."

UNIV. OF
CALIFORNIA

GENERAL VIEW OF YOSEMITE VALLEY

THE YOSEMITE VALLEY.

Silence!" Emotions new and strange here rise
And sweep with cyclonic force the breast!
A new, strange world, all-powerful and sublime,
Enchains, enslaves, and fetters all.
The greatest, most of all, are fettered most.
Only the pygmies chatter, and fools alone
Find laughter here where Nature speaks
In tones of grandeur and sublimity!
Strong lips are dumb, and eyes unused to tears
Are forced to yield the highest tribute of the soul
To these grand thoughts of the Eternal Mind!

In the golden West, where the towering mountains
    Pillow their heads on the breast of the sky,
Where the storm-king stores in his frozen fountains
    Life for the valleys, when parched and dry;
In a wonder-land, where God, in splendor,
    His thought has spoken in words of stone;
Grandeur sublime and Beauty tender
    Guard His throne.

'Mid massive domes of the Sierras' columns,
    Where power supreme to the eye is shown,
Where an awe-inspiring vastness solemns
    The mind with force of the great Unknown,
There lies a gem — a thought of beauty
    Which the mountains guard, as the depths the sea,
Where peace is law and joy is duty —
    Yosemite!

Its granite walls but the eagles follow
    To dizzying heights in the distant sky;
No eye can see from their crests the hollow
    Where in peace the beautiful valleys lie;
No foot has trod its sky-linked turrets;
    The heaven's purple enmantles them,
The crystal snows alone are for its
    Diadem.

Long ages since a glacier rested
Within these walls, and then begun
Erosion's work, 'til, of form divested —
Slowly yielding to rain and sun —
The ice-king grand, with beauty glowing,
That here on high had reared its head,
Hearing the song of the south wind blowing,
Left its bed.

These massive walls remain unheeding
The frosts of Winter, the Summer's sun;
Alone unmoved by every pleading
By Nature voiced, since time begun.
The winds, the storm, the rage volcanic,
In vain to move their structure yearns;
Jove's lance with seething hate satanic
Futile burns.

The golden rays of the sunlight, turning
The icy bolts of the vaults of snow,
Shone in, and, 'neath their kisses burning,
The gems were wooed to a crystal flow.
"River of Mercy" for all things near it,
Dispensing life with its song of glee,
White as a virgin's unsoiled spirit,
Light and free.

Swifter than winds or the flight of swallow,
The milk-white waves of this river foam
On toward the granite-guarded hollow,
Where bloom and joy find a welcome home;
With plunge and shout, like distant thunder,
It leaps from the brow of that mountain wall;
It spins and weaves and bursts asunder
In its fall.

White rockets flash from the columns' cover,
Their courses marked by a silvery mist;
Caught by the winds the spray-wreaths hover,
In folds of light by the sunbeams kissed;
Veiling the river's lips which thunder,
With sprays bejeweled and clouds high rolled;
Beauty most rare! Magical wonder,
Shot with gold!

CALIFORNIA

YOSEMITE FALLS

Vision divine, unmoved and nameless,
    Thy wonders remain while ages fret;
Thy power unfettered and ever tameless,
    Thy Bows of Promise forever set;
Now by the gold of the sunlight painted,
    Now by the rays of Night's pale bride;
Matchless work of all things created—
    Deified!

Thy castled walls, sphinx-like, forever
    Their silent story ceaseless tell,
Unto the crystal, foaming river,
    Whose tones of thunder, chimes of bell,
Voice the only thought here spoken
    Of ages past which one may know,
Heard in the words unchanged, unbroken,
    "Long ago."

Throne of the continent! Queen of all splendor!
    Creation supernal! Work wholly divine!
When touched by thy presence the cold heart grows tender,
    And reels with a joy as though drunken with wine.
Transcendent valley, with sky-woven ceiling,
    Rivers that murmur, white-lipped falls that roar,
Records divine, His wonders revealing
    More and more.

EVENING ON MT. WHITNEY.

Upon this mountain king the evening sun
Had placed a coronet of gold. The day
Had ceased from toil; adown the western way
His gorgeous cohorts paused as if to view
The matchless scene, and throw a fond farewell
To snow-crowned peak and verdure-painted vale.
Swiftly the passing moments flew between
The golden warp, unrolling from the sun,
Weaving into the woof of day bright threads,
To form the mantle which the Present gives,

Has ever given, nor will cease to give
Unto the Past 'til Time shall still his loom
And sink into oblivion. Silence,
Deep, soulful and profound with clearer sense,
Gives loftier meaning now than words convey,
For here the soul is charmed by thoughts half-formed,
To which a spoken word would be a sword,
Or, as the steel-clad hoof of trooper's horse
To newly-fallen snows or blooming flowers.

Invading cloud-land here I stood and gazed
Upon the Alpine billows far and wide—
Snow-capped, sky-mantled and cloud-swept they seemed,
Flashing resplendent 'neath the setting light,
Revealing by their silent forms of power
Such vastness as to cause my trembling soul
To sink into itself, nor dare to stand
Upon this awful brink, lest it should fall
And lose its every sense of being thus
In contemplation of its nothingness.
Thousands of peaks and domes below appeared,
And folded in between the lovely vales,
A thousand flashing streams, like silver trails,
Wound gracefully from parian-folded brow
To verdure-sandled foot of grandeur's forms.
A multitude of lakes beset the scene,
Befitting jewels for these mighty kings;
Pearls, emeralds and rubies each in turn
More beautiful appeared, as light and shade
Gave to them each a glory all its own.

The sun sunk slowly to his wonted rest,
But ere he set, his flashing swords of flame
Leaped forth and stabbed the bosom of the day
'Til sky and cloud and lofty peaks of snow
Were bathed in crimson, from the fatal wound.
The soft wind slowly winged the vales below,
Chanting, in solemn tones, a requiem.
Night softly drew her mantle o'er the scene
And golden stars kept watch until the dawn.

MY HUNTING DOG.

"Hie on, my boy!" At my command,
He speeds away with merry bound;
This way and that, by wave of hand,
He covers every foot of ground.

His feathered coat and silken ears,
(In color white and black and tan)
Fanned by the winds, a joy appears
Unto the eye of every man.

Bounding along the grassy slope,
Snuffing the air so gently blown;
He sudden halts him in his lope,
And stands as if carved out of stone.

With head half turned toward the wind,
He "points" the bird from sight secure;
Though covered in its grassy blind,
He knows its presence, prompt and sure.

One paw half raised, just where the scent
Froze every muscle of his frame;
Unending source of wonderment,
By which he says, "I've found the game."

"Steady, my boy!" And I advance,
Thrilled with the scene so dear to me;
See how his brown eyes sparkle, dance;
His attitude, expectancy.

One step again, whir-r-bir-r bang! bang!
He drops at flutter of the bird;
And while the echoing shots still rang:
"Go fetch!" He bounds away at word.

Proudly he bears the trophy in,
And yields it to my waiting hand;
Careful the word of praise to win,
There's scarce his equal in the land.

And do you wonder that I pause,
And on him words of love expend?
I always do, and that because
Man has no better, truer friend.

THE SUN-KISSED SEA.

A beauty rare, beyond compare,
Is sun-kissed sea.
No scene so calm — no scene so fair
As this to me.

When floods of light dispel the night,
The morning's kiss,
On waves which sparkle with delight,
Is loveliness.

When ends my day, I trust and pray,
My voyage be
O'er waters where some golden ray
May kiss the sea.

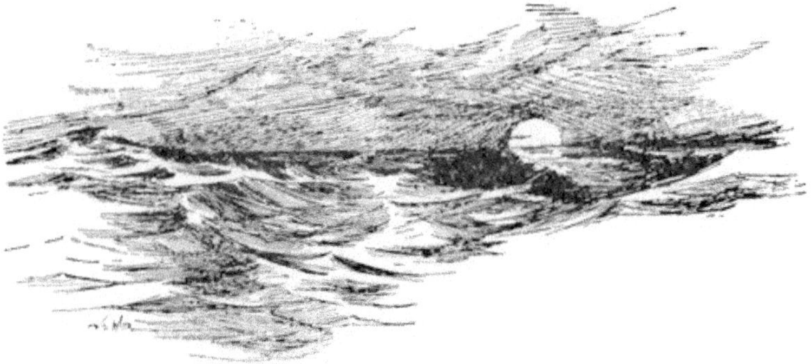

BRAMBLES AND CORN.

I would away from the city, where trouble and
discord aboundeth;
Where Pride, and Envy, and Malice with daggers
drawn lieth in wait;
Away from the slimy, coiled serpents whose anger
no warning soundeth,
Away from the pitiless tigers crouching each side
of the gate.

I would away from the falseness, the shallow and
constant dissembling —
The ill masquerading of self, the better to seize on
one's prey —
The caricatures of manhood whose natures have not
the resembling
Of aught that toucheth with honor, who love
darkness rather than day.

I would away from the fever, the restless and
anguishing burning
That throbs through my veins with unrest,
compelling the fibers to part;
I would seek me a balm and a solace for this
unceasing yearning
Which draws, like a fierce young lion, the warm
crimson blood from my heart.

But wherefore this yearning? Why make of
humanity's evils a thorn?
They are, and while mankind is human and
finite, will be;
So long as love's fondest fruition is felt in the kiss
of first-born;
So long as heaven's blue arching looks smilingly
down on the sea.

I plead no contentment with evil; unrest is the
plowshare of good,
Preparing the soul for its labor in seeking only the
light;
The hope of endless progression; the effort to be
understood;
Longing for that which is better; the cry of the
lost in the night.

Can Joy be when Harmony fleeth? Composure,
where soundeth a din?
Can one handle thistles unpricken? Touch fire, and
not feel the burn?
Drink deep at the fountains of poison, and escape
the fever within?
Does acquaintance with sin e'er quicken desire all
sinning to spurn?

Such knowledge, to most minds, is evil, and casteth
an upas-tree shade;
The pure must live in the sunlight—the sunlight of
love and of truth;
The shadow of evil will tarnish, and dwelt in, will
surely degrade,
Sapping the fountains of pleasure and searing the
beauty of youth.

Weeds ripen without cultivation; the province of
labor is plain;
Stony ground may be made fallow; the poison nut
changed to a fruit;
But patience and toil the requiring, for progress is
made but with pain;
Fruitage the end of the season, the Spring-time
presents but the root.

The brambles grow rank in the thicket, there
flourish the poisonous vines;
The fruits of the field and vineyard by long
cultivation are born;
There would be no reaping or harvest, no drinking
of life-giving wines,
If freedom from tares were unnurtured to yield us
the grapes and corn.

What though you escape the foul poisons? be
blinded to all, and yet dumb?
Evil exists as a dagger, which knowledge will
drive to your heart,
And Pity will brood you a sorrow, so sure as
to-morrow will come,
Its shadow lie heavy upon you, and never more
will it depart.

How can you escape it? How dare you? Your
duty supreme is to keep
A loving and tender surveillance over your
brother and friend,
Trusting to Him who is sleepless, when it needs be
your weary eyes sleep,
Undoubting that in the great future Peace will
crown toil in the end.

The deeds for rejoicing are fewer than those over
which we may weep,
And laughter often is echo of unseen yet heart-
rending tears;
We masquerade sorrow with smilings, the bitter is
poignant and deep;
Merriment lives but a season, while grief taketh
root for the years.

I am so weary, weary of evil, so weary of pain
and strife;
Weary of whetting and dulling the sword to be
used in the fray;
The ceaseless doing and undoing of threads in the
warp of this life.
To what end? The peace that cometh, if peace
come at close of the day.

What is life for? But to gather the dross of earth
in full measure?
To dig and to delve in the mart 'til Avarice
turns Youth to Age?
To warp the heart and the mind till they make of
dissembling a pleasure?
To record the wreckage called gain, in blood in
each line on the page?

Wherefore this unceasing, conscienceless grasping
for that which is fleeting?
This chasing of dazzling bows that dissolve like
mists in the air?
This pandering to plunder and passion, and
driving the heart to beating,
Till panting and o'erworn we languish and
Hope gives way to Despair?

For what shall it profit the miser though he the
whole world should acquire?
Will it brighten the bloom of roses, or deaden the
prick of thorn?
Will it deepen one single pleasure, or strengthen
one righteous desire?
Will it soften the glow of sunset, or brighten the
flush of morn?

The needs of the body are transient, the soul in
itself is divine;
Of earth we needs must be earthy, if wedded to
self and to gain;
The body is but an expression, symbolic and plastic
the sign;
The potence and power of the spirit beams out on
the world through the brain.

And shall we content to degrade it, to make of it
servant alone?
The King become but a vassal, a menial for
time-serving deeds?
Tossed hither and thither at random, by fierce
passion-winds rudely blown?
A camp-follower in the procession, subsisting on
husks and weeds?

The fountains of Peace and of Pleasure lie in the
line of transition,
Revealed by thoughts that tend upward and
waken desire to press on,
Inquiring of Faith the direction, making of self an
omission,
And ever praying and seeking the roseate flush of
the dawn.

ON SEEING A ROSEBUD IN THE STREET.

I saw a rosebud in the street,
 Where it had carelessly been tossed;
Just where a thousand passing feet
 Were treading, when the way they crossed.

It pained me much this flower to see,
 Trodden and crushed into the slime;
It seemed to cry appealingly
 Against the cold, unfeeling crime.

For it is crime and nothing less,
 Aught of the beautiful to crush;
The lack of heart — the soullessness —
 Shown by the crowd should cause a blush.

And then I thought, oh, deeper shame!
 That Truth should prompt me to relate
Of crimes too dark to have a name,
 Wereby pure souls meet such a fate.

THE DESTRUCTION OF POMPEII.

When first the infant Morn stirred on his couch
And lit the Orient with grayish light,
Bidding his radiant heralds to announce,
In brighter gleams, the coming of that day,
He knew the glorious sun would look upon
No fairer scene, in all the circling orbit of his course,
Than Pompeii, nestled on the bay, at foot
Of grandest mountain in all Italy.

The day-god mounted up his shining way
And, looking on that city fair, beheld
A brilliant scene of pomp and pageantry.
The blare of trumpets and the sound of horns
Was heard through all its busy streets, and beat
Against the dome of heaven with their blasts.
The populace in holiday attire,
Hither and thither ran, intent on deeds
Of needed preparation for the day;
A day, they thought, of revels and of sports—

Such sports as savage breasts delight, and move
To quicker beatings hearts, most hard and stern;
For on this day, as was the custom then,
The prisoners and such as pleased the king
To sacrifice for trespass of his will,
Were to be led into the arena,
For the ferocious beasts to feed upon,
While all the fierce Campanians looked on.

The wild beasts roared within their prison cells,
Where, for long days, without the taste of food,
They had been kept, that hunger sharpen keen
Their thirst for human blood, and render all
Their deep forocity more horrible!
The multitude assembles: scarce less fierce
Are they than the wild beasts, whose angry roars
They greet with loud and eager shouts of joy!
Each face a canvas on which Passion throws
His strongest limnings of ferocity!
Tutored in war and used to scenes of blood,
Hardened in cruelty, and conscienceless
Of all emotions which are akin to grace!
Lost, and thrice damned with every curse that hell
Metes out to those who trample Heaven's law.
All here assembled are athirst for blood!
Warm, human blood, spilled by the lion's power!
Victims, defenseless and alone, they joy
To see, by wild beasts rent — torn limb from limb!
The while that life doth linger, hear their cries —
Cries that should freeze the life-blood in its course,
And render dumb all sound from human lips,
Save Horror's shrieks and Pity's wailing groans.
But o'er such scenes, these bestial fiends but laugh,
And, filling chalices of fresh, warm blood,
They drink to soul of Nero, Nero! King!
And rend the heavens with their loud acclaim,
In honor of his many butcheries.

Full times and oft had they assembled thus
To witness such wild carnivals of blood.
The amphitheatre for this was made,
A temple for these cruel scenes of death!

Scenes, black as malice and malignant hate
Combined, could e'er devise to feed upon!
The king and all his royal court looked on,
And cursed or cheered as it befit their moods,
Commenting on the wild and angry beasts
As they leaped forth and crouched about the walls.
Selecting those of fiercest gaze, whose eyes
Most fiercely shone with light of hungry fire,
They said: "This beast will make a glorious war!
And that will lose no time to glut his maw
With human blood." And wagers laid they all
Upon the contest; but as to beasts alone,
For the poor men were victims all foredoomed.

See! now the beasts have scented out their prey!
They crouch and crawl toward the terrored men;
Soft-footed they, and noiseless of approach;
But oh, their eyes! how luminous and fierce!
Darting a constant gleam of burning fire.
Now crouching low, they all prepare to spring;
Their great forms quiver, and they lash their tails,
One instant more, now! now! The throng awaits,
With bated breath, the final spring, when, lo!
The earth was shaken as a reed in storm!
Each heart was filled with terror, and each face
Grew ghastly white at thought of coming doom.
The wild beasts, filled with dread, approached the men
And licked their hands! Crouched at their feet in fear,
And seemed as if to crave of them a shield!

The sea becalmed as though its powers were dead;
The air ceased breathing, and a murky hue
Spread o'er the heavens as a veil to hide
From others' eyes that city's awful doom.
The earth rose and fell like ocean billows;
The city's masonries were overthrown
And tossed about as though but eider-down!
The heavens burst into a sea of flame
As Mount Vesuvius, erstwhile so calm,
Belched forth the mighty billows of his ire,
Which rolled, a burning sea, adown his form

And, like mammoth rockets, shot across the sky,
Pouring great flaming cataracts of fire
Upon that city's all defenceless head!

In wildest terror those who could, now fled;
Each praying unto all, for help and aid.
The terror swept away all barriers,
And kings from vassals humbly craved a boon!
Affrighted through the streets they shrieking ran,
Seeking for safety, and yet finding none.
The amphitheatre — the city's pride,
Opened its mighty walls and trembling fell,
Crushing beneath its ponderous form the throng.
The rolling, dashing, hissing sea of fire,
Like the great billows of the deep, in storm,
Rolled through its streets and from the heavens fell,
Until beneath the molten waves it lay
A corpse, whose cause of death became its tomb.

THINGS TO LOVE.

I love all beauty, let it be
In sky, or flower, or leafy tree,
In babbling brook or humming bee;
I love it well,
When sunset on the calm, blue sea
Casts Beauty's spell.

All Nature speaks of beauties rare;
In every cloud that floats in air,
And all around us, everywhere,
Will we but see
The master hand of beauty there —
Divinity!

THE ANGELS OF SHILOH

(A FRAGMENT)

AN IDYL OF THE GREAT REBELLION

THE ANGELS OF SHILOH.

OH, fair is the land where the sun brightly shines,
Where the palmettoes grow and the tall, stately pines
Rear aloft their proud heads to the soft, mellow skies,
Wafting back to the sea its low, murmuring sighs.
Where the richest fruits ripen, and fairest of flowers
Eternally bloom, amid sylvan-like bowers;
Where the nightingale's music at twilight is heard,
And the heart by the beauties of nature is stirred;
Where birds of gay plumage fill forest and grove,
And balmy winds whisper of music and love;
Where the magnolia blooms, fairest flower 'neath the sky;
The wealth of its beauty with Eden's might vie;
Where the orange, the lemon, the fig and the palm,
Hath laden the air with the wealth of their balm.
Here, here short of heaven, I would choose me to dwell,
And drink deep of the joys which no language can tell,
For the gods of the land, and the gods of the sea,
Have lavished, sweet Southland, their affections on thee.
If a spot on the earth may be found whereon bliss
Is borne full on each breeze, it is this, it is this.
The light of her mornings, when o'er the sea streaming
In ripples of radiance brilliant and fair,
Steals soft on the eyelids of sleepers there dreaming,
And wakes them with breath of perfume on the air.
The sweet, wooing kiss of her breezes at night;
The light of her moon's witching beams as they fall
In a shimmering veil of soft silvery light,
When cast in their magical splendor o'er all,
Form a scene, once beheld, time can never efface,
For no other can vie with its beauty and grace.

Sweet land of enchantment, how balmy and tender
Are all of the breezes which over thee blow;
The scent of thy roses, how sweetly they render
The breath of thy gardens to mortals below!

At quiet hours of even-tide,
Here lovers o'er her silver lakes
In light canoes so softly glide,
The waves scarce tremble in their wakes;
And golden stars seem angel-eyes,
As through the purpling shroud of night
These liquid mirrors of the skies
Reflect their glories to the sight.
With sky, and moon, and stars above,
And stars, and moon, and sky below,
They fondly breathe their vows of love,
In ecstasies no heart may know
That hath not breathed, that hath not seen
These Eden spots elysian.
And when the orb of day sheds bright
His lustrous rays of golden light,
The purpling arches of the sky
Unfathomed in their beauty lie;
Where feathery cloudlets, slow of wing,
Float dreamily those sky-seas o'er,
Seeking no port, no anchoring,
Their seas alone hath not a shore.
Here, when all else is calm and still,
Nightly complains the whip-poor-will;
While on each breeze, at eve and morn,
The lily blows its scented horn.

Soft-footed Spring through Shiloh's wood
Came in her fair young motherhood
To bless the earth with offspring fair,
And peace to all the world declare.
All, all with animation rife
Bespoke the full high tide of life.
Fresh flowers and grasses quickly spring
From out the brown earth's covering;
The skies became a deeper blue,

AT QUIET HOUR OF EVEN-TIDE

UNIV. OF
CALIFORNIA

The clouds took on a richer hue,
The air was soft as mother's kiss,
Enamored of her loveliness,
While peace on every breeze was borne;
The waving grass, the budding thorn,
The opening leaf, the clinging vine
Which round the great trees closely twine;
The blushing rose, the violet blue,
Now springing up, still sweeter grew
With smile of sun and tear of dew.

Refreshing life, at every breath
Was on each breeze; no sign of death
O'er Nature's lovely form and face
Could eye most searching find a trace,
As over all those wooded hills
The morning sunlight softly streamed,
Lighting her veils and purling rills,
And on the river brightly gleamed;
While in her tented city sleeping,
Thousands of noble soldiers lay,
Who ere the sun should set that day
Would pass all sorrow and all weeping,
Ere faded its bright light away.
Little they thought in hours of waking
That lovely morn would be their last;
That while its peaceful light was breaking,
Death's sombre wing was o'er them cast.
'Twas eve of battle, yet no fears
Came to the loyal volunteers;
No thought had they of dangers nigh,
No clouds bedimmed their sunny sky;
Beguiled with pleasure and with song,
The gloaming hours there passed along;
A peaceful camp, where joy and mirth,
Each moment found a welcome birth;
Amid the wooded hills they lay,
As though 'twere but a holiday.
About the camp-fires, brightly gleaming,
They stories told of peace and love,
And kindness from each eye was beaming—
The eagle ruled less than the dove.

Serenely calm the silver moon
Betook her way across the sky,
As sleep, the blessed, restful boon,
Kissed gently down the weary eye;
And golden stars resplendent shone
With gleaming rays upon the earth,
And soft winds gently, sweetly blown
Told of the Spring-time floweret's birth.
All nature sought with peace to bless
Where'er on earth was wretchedness,
And not a care to them was known —
God's footstool seemed, that night, His throne!

'Twas Sabbath morn, and from the East
The heralds of her coming break
Upon the rest of night, and wake
Her sleepers there; bid them away
Before the hosts of coming day.

For lo! Aurora rises now,
With folds of purple on her brow,
Her form enwrapped in folds of light,
Unto the gods a pleasing sight,
As, with red sandals shod, lo! she
Comes dripping from the morning sea,
To rule the day in majesty.
Pure as the soul of infant's prayer
Is wave of that sweet morning air —
The breath of Spring is everywhere.
All nature moved by her sweet kiss,
Arrayed in gorgeous loveliness,
Mirrored in flower, and tree, and sod,
The loving smile of Nature's god.

Sweet Sabbath day, of all most blessed,
For peace and prayer and quiet rest;
When thoughts of love to fellow man
Affection's fires most strive to fan;
When hearts to God do most aspire
To banish thoughts of gross desire,
And nature purify by prayer.

AURORA

The tuneful birds poured forth their lay
To welcome dawn of coming day;
With cheery song, each feathered throat
Poured on the balmy air, to float,
Rich notes which sweetly sped along
A harmony of pulsing song,
In which was heard no note of pain,
No sad lament, no weird refrain,
But melody of joy alone
Was breathed in every tuneful tone,
Bidding all hearts rejoice again,
As doth the verdant hill and plain
In golden sunshine after rain.

While ashen fingers of the morn
Were seeking in the East to free
The hills from mantles they had worn
Of sombre night's weird drapery,
By plucking here and there a star,
From out the dome of Heaven's arch,
That fair Aurora meet no bar
While sweeping upward in her march—
Before her dazzling smile be given,
To wake the earth and light the heav'n,
The rebel foes their banners flung
Upon the morning's gloaming air—
In silence marched the hills among,
In solid columns waited there,
But for the morning's light to show
The path which lay toward their foe,
That with its first effulgent gleams
They might dash through the wooded hills,
And wake to death, from peaceful dreams,
The camps that lay by stream and rills.

The eagles rest when cloudless skies
O'erarch their lofty, craggy nests,
And balmy winds, like peaceful sighs,
Lull to repose their powerful breasts;
But when the tempests madly rise,
And every power of earth defies,
Hurling with vengeance through the air

The voice of wild destruction there;
Then rouse they from their quiet dream,
And mingle their loud, piercing scream
With voice of heaven's bursting cloud,
However fierce, and deep, and loud;
And to the lightning's gleaming ire,
They answer with an eye of fire,
And soar aloft, on powerful wing,
To meet the storm-king's challenging,
Priding themselves in strength to prove,
Their power to mount the storms above!
So with the loyal, peaceful men;
When first the cloud of war arose,
It woke the fire within them then,
To meet the nation's deadly foes;
And to the world they quickly prove,
No force so great as that of love.
Each peaceful home proved a defence
Of greater strength and consequence
Unto the nation, in the hour
When discord's voice broke into war,
Than standing armies e'er could be,
Because of love's true loyalty.

They woke, when first the day was born,
As faintly flushed the East with morn;
While opening rose and budding thorn,
        Sweet censers there,
Swung to and fro with breath of Spring,
As to her revelry they bring
Rich odors which they freely fling
        Upon the air.

The purpling hue of coming day
Was softly turning into gray,
Before the sun's first glowing ray;
        When from the South,
In thunder tones there swift arose
A voice that frightened all repose,
The voice of death, that fiercely glows
        From cannon's mouth.

And none may know who did not see
That awful sight of misery,
The trials of those who fought to free,
With might and main,
The flag to us our fathers gave,
The flag that floats above the brave,
The flag that thousands died to save
From treason's stain.

Amid the surging billows there,
Death rode on Terror through the air,
And to the heart brought wild despair
With every breath;
Where fell their loyal comrades 'round,
Their hearts' blood dyeing all the ground,
The sky surcharged with awful sound
Of woe and death;
Yet, braving all the dangers there,
They kept the Old Flag in the air.

In the fore of the fight where the death billows rolled,
And the crimson flood flowed from the breast of the bold,
'Mid the hissing of bullets and scream of the shell,
In the heat of the charge where our loyal men fell,
Where the peal of the batteries thundered and roared,
Where the bayonets clashed, and the keen, flashing sword
Struck deep to the hearts of the noble men there,
Our loyal boys kept the Old Flag in the air.

When the thunders were fierce, and the rage of the storm
Would cause them to waver, they quickly would form
On a line where their colors were kissing the air,
For they knew every able, true soldier was there
With a heart for endeavor, that knew not a fear,
For to every brave soldier the Old Flag was dear —
Aye, sacred to him as the breath of a prayer,
And he'd gladly die keeping that flag in the air.

Though the war-bees flew thick with their sharp, piercing sting,
Round the spot where it stood, yet their murderous ring
Deterred not brave men its bright folds to still fly,
A menace to traitors, high up in the sky.

Though they threw on its bearer the heat of their fire,
And strove it to humble with fierce, venomed ire;
Though the hazard was great the loved colors to bear,
Yet they kept, through it all, the Old Flag in the air.

When a color-man fell, quick another would seize
The standard, and fling the old flag to the breeze;
No pausing for danger, no counting the cost,
A life was as nothing to the flag being lost!
For as comrades were fighting its loved folds to free,
All over the land and all over the sea,
The last words they whispered, as they fell dying there,
Was: "Boys, keep the Old Flag still high in the air."

No scene that mortal man may know
Can equal that of charging foe;
And here it came with all of dread
To which war's hurricane is wed.
The bravest hearts were most appalled,
While comrades to each other called:
"Wake, brothers, wake! O, wake and see
The awful grandeur of the storm;
The woods, like billows of the sea,
Sway back and forth resistlessly;
Like blades or grass, lo! every tree
Bows low its proud and stately form.
The leaves before the fiery blast
In whirling eddies swift are cast,
And twigs and limbs are hurling fast,
Borne on the wild storm's scorching breath,
In every movement speaking death."

While swarming thick the war bee's wing
To every spot their deadly sting;
The sky is darkened by the breath
Of these wild messengers of death,
While ears are dumb to every sound,
Save that of war, which all around
Leaps through the terror-stricken air,
As all its voices, fierce, declare
The reign of Terror everywhere.

See, from the edge of yonder wood
Ten thousand gleaming blades of steel!
With charging yell, that chills the blood,
The enemy's great columns wheel,
And dashing down the steep incline,
With all of mortal power combine.
To drive from out their chosen stand
Our comrades' brave and loyal band.
What! have they fled? is no defence
Now to be made against the foe?
Gods! what a sound the heavens rend!
From center to circumference,
The trembling earth rocks to and fro,
As wild Destruction's forces blend
In one appalling burst of woe!

See! See! they fall and helpless writhe,
As grass before the reaper's scythe.
With all of human strength and power,
They are but dry reeds in this hour,
Before the raging battle's tide,
Which seems to grow more deep and wide,
With flash of sword, and roar of gun,
As though the Fates would soon decide:
The victory be lost or won.

Mars, in his chariot of fire,
Now madly dashes wildly on,
As with a scowl of vengeful ire,
He plies his scourge with fierce desire,
The raging tempest to outrun!
While Flight and Terror madly fly
Across the smoke-beclouded sky,
Leaping affrighted through the air,
While, flowing out behind, his hair
Is fanned to streaming shreds of flame,
As on, still on, they swiftly dash
Amid the deafening roar and crash,
Where Pity lives, but in a name.
All helpless 'neath their powerful feet,
They trample, crush, in sore defeat,
And render Pluto's reign complete,

As to destruction quick are hurl'd
All things that would oppose,
And, terror-stricken, from the world
Escape, alone in death, his foes.
His form was like storm-clouds at night,
And ruin was his soul's delight;
His breath was death to all the land,
Deep woe his footsteps e'er attend;
While nations trembled, empires fell,
For all his ways turn peace to hell!

Hark to the screaming of the shell,
As through the wood it onward flies;
Mark the wild havoc where it fell —
All life around it withered lies.
Another, and another, see,
Striking of sound the highest key,
In war's wild song of jubilee.
The solid shot goes crashing on
With wild, terrific, awful force,
Blasting within its murderous course
All here beneath the smiling sun.
Hark to the groaning of the trees!
As 'neath the wound of cannon ball,
Like withered grass before the breeze,
They snap and in confusion fall.

Here, 'midst the storm of battle, stood
Love's sweet expression — womanhood.
Strong in affection's powerful might,
Unshrinking at the awful sight,
Through lonely hours of dreary night,
As with the soul of love imbued,
She shrank not at the sight of blood.
With Beauty's form and Love's sweet face,
Combining with the purest grace,
All human strength and loveliness.
Aye! more than human love we see,
The soul of woman's sympathy
Is Heaven's true Divinity;
And to the wounded soldier there,
Who on that battle field was lying,

She came, an angel pure and fair,
To sooth his troubled heart when dying.
If each could speak again to-day,
They would rejoice with me to say:
The hand of woman, oh, how sweet,
Upon the battle-field to meet;
Her voice is music to the soul,
Her touch is balm for every pain,
The surges cease within to roll,
At her command peace smiles again.

A prayer ascended on each breath,
That sweet relief might come in death;
For death to them a boon would be,
Compared to this deep misery;
For spirit of the Raven Wing
Alone hath now the power to bring
Relief from such dire suffering.
Oh! must life's fluid, drop by drop,
Ooze from their wounds until it stop,
For that the fount of life be dry,
And pale the lip and glazed the eye?
Must every sense of heart and brain
Be tortured to its highest strain,
And all the agony and woe,
That human heart may ever know,
Be wrung from out the tortured frames,
Which burn with all the hellish flames
That human agony can give,
And yet the wretched victims live?

Unconsciousness at times was given,
And with it came a glimpse of Heaven.
Visions of cool and shady dells,
Where bloomed the scented pampernells,
O'erhung with cypress and with vine,
Whose leaves and tendrils intertwine
And form, beneath the brazen sky,
A sweet and pleasant canopy,
Where, stealing from the moss-grown nook,
Laughing in merry, gleeful mood,
Comes gushing the refreshing brook,

Which glides away amid the wood.
Could heaven give to earth its bliss,
For these poor souls, it would be this.
When senses fade, the pain grows less,
By reason of unconsciousness,
Which, stealing o'er the weary brain,
Relieves them of their racking pain.

Poor, suffering souls, never again
Shall love's sweet gleaming smile repay
Thy hearts for this deep, bitter pain,
That racks thy helpless forms to-day;
No more shall love's bright, golden head,
Be pillowed on each manly breast,
To-morrow's sun shall find thee dead,
Thy troubled forms shall be at rest,
Beneath the damp and quiet sod,
While wings thy spirits on to God;
Yes on, still on, forever on!
For, unto the immortal soul,
Heaven, for aye, shall be a dawn,
While vast Eternity shall roll.
When mortal sense had closed, their eyes
Beheld the glow of Paradise;
A glory, which no human soul
Can know or see,
Till kindly, Death shall backward roll
Mortality.
And then their souls, with sense unrolled,
Developed twice ten-thousandfold,
Their upward flight, from star to star,
'Mid luminous depths of radiance far,
Shall find their ever widening sense
A center still, while all around,
To growing sight and waking sound,
Is measureless circumference.

As on, still on, they upward glide,
The gates of Heaven still open wide,
And as they freely backward swing,
They hear the gladsome voices ring

A welcome, in sweet unison,
From angels brighter than the sun,
Whose gleaming forms of radiant light,
Would blind and dazzle mortal sight.

There all that human love had known,
Had to celestial beauty grown;
Each thing of beauty on the earth,
Is given there immortal birth.
The birds, the flowers, the lakes, and rills,
All things, the heart with gladness fills.
The thought of age, the form of youth,
The love of beauty, and of truth,
There grows and widens with each breath,
And nothing knows or thinks of death;
For over his dread skeleton
They each and all have victory won.
Hope holds not out a promise vain,
No thought can come of grief or pain,
Their sun of joy shall never set,
Ne'er fall the shadow of regret;
But light, and bliss, and peace is there,
With all that renders life most fair,
Added to Imortality,
Their every gift the gods have given,
With ample power and liberty,
To taste the sweetest joys of Heaven.

On, on with easy motion grace,
They wing their way through azure space,
While soft winds, laden with perfume,
Caught from celestial flowers that bloom
In spirit gardens of the free,
To gladden Immortality,
Reveal new beauties as they rise,
And Heaven prove one glad surprise.
In that bright land of radiant bliss,
Where all is joy and loveliness,
Where peace and purity are born,
And glows for aye the flush of morn.
With beaming rays of light forever,
That form a glist'ning, pulsing sea,

Upon whose bosom, shining ever,
Flow waves of sweetest melody.
Bathed in celestial beauty there
The mountains rise the sky to kiss,
While that soft, balmy, ambient air
Is angels' breath, compared to this;
While on the Tree of Life there grows,
Rich fruits, which every bough is bending;
Which burden every wind that blows
With sweetest odors of their lending;
A perfect sweetness to the store
Of all the lovely offerings given,
By all the gods who freely pour,
Their richest bounties into Heaven.
And music, sweet of glory, fills
All airy space and gently trills,
Through the illimitable dome,
Wherever space or substance roam,
To every part, where'er it lie,
Of measureless Eternity.

As sunlight fills our sky at day,
And beams with soft and pulsing ray,
Beyond, above all human sight,
Or sense of sound, its melody,
Flows in rich waves there constantly.
While onward still their starry flight,
Beyond the shadows of the night,
They swift pursue their upward way,
To Heaven's light of endless day.
Through constellation of the sun
Their speedy flight is quickly run,
Through gleams of light thrown from afar,
Then through the shadow of a star,
The one called day, the other night,
To mortals' dim, contracted sight;
Their visions widen and they see
And understand all mystery.

Millions of worlds above, below,
Within their circling orbits go,
Through purpling mists of airy sea,

Moving in perfect harmony;
And thus have moved through countless years,
To pulsing music of the spheres.
Through vast expanse of endless space,
Unknown, unbound, and measureless;
Through fields of bright, eternal day,
They still pursue their onward way.

Oh, pure and sweet is everything,
The flowers that bloom, the birds that sing,
The soul that wakes to life the leaf,
Which ne'er shall know a fading grief.
The winds that softly, sweetly blow,
The low voiced rivers' peaceful flow;
The friendly grasp of love's warm hand,
That long has passed from mortal land;
Ten thousand joys that only rise,
Within the gates of Paradise,
Come to their ever waking sense
With touch so thrilling and intense,
That every breath was sweetest bliss,
Unto the hungry, waking soul,
As lovers' sweet, fond virgin kiss,
In waves of pleasure o'er them roll.

Beautiful world where is no gloom,
No death, no sorrow, and no tomb,
No pain, no sickness, and no tears,
No woe, no bitterness, no fears,
No wars, no envyings, no strife,
But sweet and peaceful is the life
Of all who pass its gates within,
Absolved from every touch of sin;
Where love, and joy, and peace divine,
To crown life's pleasures all combine;
The gentle music of the spheres,
Keep time with golden flood of years,
And newer, deeper pleasures rise,
As God reveals some new surprise.
Still on they upward rise, and see
The beauties of life's mystery;

The human heart, its doubts and fears,
Its joys, its sorrows, and its tears,
Its virtues, and its troubling sins,
And all without us and within,
Why we are weak, and blind, and chained,
Is fully to all there explained.

Then for the dead, why mourn and weep?
Their life is sweeter far than sleep,
For to their souls alone is given
The power to taste the joys of Heaven.
We should but weep for those who still
Bear yet life's burdens up the hill ;
The lone, and blind, and halt, and poor,
Who wait the swinging of death's door,
That shall admit them into rest,
From this life's mournful wretchedness.

Down in a glen, where a willow tree bending
Over the banks of a brooklet below,
Lay a young soldier who fell in defending
The stars and the stripes from the hand of the foe:
Fell with a murderous wound in his breast,
From out which his life-blood gushed into the stream,
Moaned, as the sun slowly sunk to the West,
And knew it was saying "farewell" with its gleam.
He thought : "I shall die by this brook all alone,
And no one shall know of my fate evermore.
Could I hear one kind voice—one loved human tone—
I ask of the gods but this one favor more,
To send to my mother one fond, loving kiss,
And a lock, if I might, of this tangled hair,
To tell her how much her sweet smile I miss,
And how I now long for her true, loving care;
I would willingly die, content to have given
My life for my country, my God, and my heaven."
Just then, as in answer unto his low sighing,
There came a soft footstep, and down by his side
There knelt a fair woman, who saw he was dying,
To comfort his soul in its sorrow she tried.

She saw by his fast-dimming eye
That death's approach was very nigh;
His mortal sun was sinking low,
His spirit struggled now to free
Itself from prison bars below,
And fly to Immortality.
He roused him then, as from a dream,
As fell the day's departing gleam,
And said to her: "I feel, and know,
My spirit hence must shortly go;
But ere it passes quite away
From mortal life, I fain would say
One parting word for those I love,
My heart's devotion still to prove
Constant as yon bright gleaming star,
Whose ray, undimmed, shines on forever,
Though mortal senses changing are
As wavelets on yon rolling river.

"Tell my father and my mother,
That their pride shall ever be
That I died, like many another
Loyal son, for liberty.
Tell my brother and my sister,
Should you e'er on earth them meet,
That I died with Heaven's vista,
Glowing brightly at my feet;
And that death no terrors brought me,
As I yielded up my breath,
That its throbbing, soulful, bright sea,
Brought me not a chilling death.

"But to her, my love, I fear it
Will for her be lone and drear,
It will kill her now to hear it;
She whose cheek has known no tear,
Save the tear she shed at parting,
And whose heart has known no pain,
Save the pain, that through it darting
With thought, I might not come again.

"Sweet lady, could I speak again
To her the thoughts which rend my heart,
'Twould be that she might know no pain —
Not e'en the shade of sorrow's dart.

"I would that life for her might be
As peaceful as a Summer sea,
Where soft winds breathing with the tide
Should woo her ship to smoothly glide,
With easy motioned swan-like grace,
Where clouds of storm should ne'er displace
The mirrored smile of Heaven's face.
Oh, may she feel my presence there,
Though viewless in the quiet air,
For by the hope of Heaven above
I will return and dwell with her,
Proving that power of human love
Defies the gloomy sepulcher.

"Tell her in hope to calmly gaze
Upon yon bright and gleaming star,
Through purpling mists its golden rays
Speak of the glories from afar.
Tell her that soon the storm of grief
Shall pass away, and sweet relief
Shall fill her soul as sorrow dies,
At thought of love's sweet memories.
Tell her, I sorrow for my fate,
Alone for that it doth relate
Unto her own, and thus should be
To her one thought of misery.

"I fain would live to feel and know
The perfect joy of loving so,
When I might shield from every storm
Her gentle heart and angel form.
And say that her sweet words of love
Have helped me bear this bitter pain,
That her inspiring spirit strove
And nerved my arm to strike again!
If I have won a crown of fame,
It should bear her inspiring name;
To her alone let praise be sung,

On her the purple robe be flung;
For, by the gods! I swear 'twas she
Who led the charge to victory!

"No power to mortal man is known,
From God's green footstool to His throne,
That can compare in force, or prove
An equal power to woman's love.
It was, it is, shall be my sun,
'Til sands of life are fully run;
If it continue not to be
I wish not immortality."

His voice grew weak, he faintly smiled,
As though some thought his pain beguiled,
As, stealing gently through his brain,
'Twould woo him back to life again.
But no; the curtains of his eyes
Are slowly, gently drooping down;
His head upon her bosom lies,
Her ringlets form a golden crown
Around that radiant face and brow,
Which glow with soul-kissed beauty now.
Behold! he starts! his eager sight
Expressing wonder and delight,
As if beholding some glad scene.
He cries: "She comes, my own, loved queen!"
In joyful tones, he echoes o'er,
"She comes, my own, forever more!"
His soul then found a sweet release,
And o'er his form stole perfect peace.

And it was true; the very hour
His soul withdrew from mortal power,
The maiden of his bosom's choice,
As if her soul had heard his voice
Calling it then from earth away,
Unlocked its prison house of clay;
And, sweetly thus, they hand in hand
Strayed into Heaven's holy land.
Then glancing o'er the battle ground,
With manly forms all thickly strewn,

She wept to think that death had found
A cause to blight them at their noon.
And weeping o'er the loyal dead,
These words of sad lament she said:

"Farewell, brave souls, forever rest
In fields of light, supremely blessed,
Beyond the power of pain or grief,
Where finds the soul a sweet relief,
Amid the joys around God's throne,
Where only peace and love are known;
Where sorrow's shadows ne'er can come
To mar that bright celestial home;
Where false, delusive hope no more
Shall rise to beck thee from the shore,
And lure thee on the ocean's wave,
With promise false as Siren's song,
And bring thee to an early grave
Ere thy pure hearts hath known a wrong.

"Farewell to thee, a fond farewell,
For joys await thy spirits there;
I would not hold thee here to dwell
Amid this pestilential air.
For when I look upon the earth,
And see the wretchedness and woe,
I would withdraw the power of birth,
And deem man blessed in doing so.
Eternal sleep a boon would be—
A pure and calm, unbroken sea,
Wherein no life should wake again,
If with it came remorse and pain.
Oh! better this, far better, far,
Than life with dreadful scenes of war!"

Here stagnant pools of water creep,
And wretched hearts in sorrow weep,
As all the ills the heart may know
Are blended in one hell of woe,
Where black despair e'er hovers o'er
The sea of night without a shore;
Where deadly serpents crawl and hiss
In all their loathsome hideousness.

Here misery the heart appalls,
And gleam of sunlight never falls;
Or, if it falls, its cheerfulness,
Contrasted with this deep distress,
Makes misery nigh measureless.
Oh, dreadful scene! how sadness flings
Her dewy mantle from her wings,
Like mist her veils of sorrow fall,
And mournfully each waking strain
Sobs in its weirdness over all,
As though no thought could cheer again.

The very rays of tim'rous light,
Seem loth to pierce the shroud of night,
And with their power to sight reveal,
To hearts that yet can mourn, and feel
The horrors of this scene around,
Where death has walked the battle ground;
A blasted garden, fearful doom!
For all its wondrous flowers had shed
Their every blossom, and the tomb
Of winter over them had spread
Its howling tempest, and its kiss
Had wrought with fierce destructiveness.

Oh, Hellish war! thy footsteps know
No tread save on the human heart,
From which the crimson wine must flow
To feed thy black and cruel art;
Thou livest but on death and pain,
And fiercely drink warm human blood,
And toast thy health full oft again
From out the heart's warm crimson flood,
And laugh when thy poor victims lie
Writhing in mortal agony;
Thou seasonest thy wine with tears,
From widows' torn and bleeding hearts,
And scoff at helpless orphans' fears,
While sharper grow thy cruel darts;
Till every crime beneath the sun
That Hell may furnish, man may know,
In thy dread name alone may run
In one great, surging sea of woe.

THE LOVERS OF SHILOH.

WHEN Peace, sweet angel, ruled the land,
And showered her gifts on every hand,
Of jeweled moments for each hour
And every hour of all the day,
Pregnant with richness and with power,
Rolled on beneath her magic sway,
She scattered there for each and all
Love's magic wreath and coronal.
And falling o'er the peaceful scene,
A wreath of flowers and myrtle green
Adorned a bosom, sweet as May,
And 'neath her ardent glances lay.
There, blushing deep, the passion rose,
Upon this maiden's bosom lying,
Sought all its fragrance to disclose
Unto her heart, while it was dying.
Kissing the rose, her lovely lips
Blushed red, while thrilled her finger tips,
As through her gentle bosom warm
Arose sweet passion's heaving storm,
As all around her, everywhere,
Sweet incense rose upon the air;
The magic odor Cupid flings
Upon us, from his downy wings,
When first we hear, so faint and low,
The twanging of his magic bow,
Or, mark the flutter of the heart
When first 'tis piercéd by his dart.
So sweet Arzelia heard and felt,
When like a spotless, snow-white dove

ARZELIA

Waking within her bosom dwelt
The image of her loyal love.
To souls like hers there come at times,
Visions of brighter, purer climes;
Voices that speaking from the air
A higher life than this declare;
Discoursing in a sweeter tone
Than to the common mortal known,
Music so soft, so sweet, and low,
The cadence of its rippling flow
Wakes not, though falling on our ear,
The power within our souls to hear.
To ėyes like her's there often rise,
The beauties bright of Paradise.
To her this power was freely given
For she was less of earth than Heaven.

And full oft "her high-born kinsmen" clustered round her in the air,
Peopling all her lovely visions with sweet radiant forms most fair,
And the waving of their pinions seemed to rustle round and o'er,
As the future life seemed swinging wide to her its mystic door.

When Autumn winds in sighing strewed the ground with withered leaves,
And all nature sobbing faintly o'er the death of Summer grieves,
And the Gheber's god in splendor slowly to the Westward rolls,
She walked alone with spirits and held converse sweet with souls.

And the gladness on the features of the loved ones that return,
Seemed to lift the clouds of sadness, seemed to cool the flames that burn,
And to fill her soul with rapture, while the radiance round her glows,
As she listened to the music, which from souls redeeméd flows.

Behold how lovely, graceful, free,
This pledge of immortality;
Pure woman straight from Paradise,
Whose glance from soulful, waking eyes,
Tells of the love that in them lies;
Immortal, far the greater part,
The mortal heaven's wondrous art,
Imperishable glory there,
Caught from the upper fields of air;
The soul, the light, the life, the love,

All aspirations from above,
Which tend to lead us up and on
To immortality's bright dawn;
Pledge of affection, pure and free,
Immortal in mortality.
And on a king of human kind
Love's brilliant, flashing coronal
Was placed to brighten all his mind,
As o'er his life its bright rays fall.
Then they two met, and knew the earth
Held not a joy of passing worth,
Unless its pleasures hence should be
Enjoyed by them in unity.
All earth was bright, the sweet birds sung
To them a purer melody,
As waves of liquid music flung
From bosom of some mystic sea
That kiss and murmur to the shore,
And, in sweet accents, o'er and o'er
Their tale of love do constant pour
Through golden years eternally.
And each to each was breath of flowers,
And when apart Old Time became
Decrepit, blind, and halt, and lame,
And, heavy shod with lead, his feet
Seemed motionless, and some few hours
For him to measure out complete
Were to their hearts full rounded years,
With Spring of laughter, hope and tears,
And Summer's sunny settled weather,
And Autumn's premonition, whether
The golden circlet of their love
Would shelter 'gainst stern Winter prove.

As sparkling streams from distant hills
Meet in the valleys at their feet,
And all the air with music fills
With cheerful murmurs as they meet,
And there unite, fore'er to run,
Two brilliant streams join into one.
So with their love; it flowed so sweet
That every day of all the year

Fresh flowers and grasses 'neath their feet
Sprang ever brightly, and no tear
Of sorrow came to dim their way,
And life to them was always May,
And every sound a low love-tune,
With blooming flowers and breath of June.
And how or why a chilling cloud
Should drift across their perfect sky
I doubt if they — leastwise not I —
Could ever tell; but so it came,
And angry flashes of hot flame
Burst o'er them, and the air grew chill,
And bitter words were quickly said;
For indignation's angry thrill
Filled both their hearts ere it had fled;
And then they parted hastily,
Each being from the other free.
Then, in the heat of passion's flame,
He wrote upon the list his name
As one of those who gave their all
In answer to their country's call —
And in a day his regiment
Into the battle line was sent.

Heavy his heart, and troubled clouds arose,
Bereaving him of rest and all repose —
The bitter thorn of life eclipsed the rose.
And not a breath of sweetness for him there
Floated upon the balmy Spring-time air;
The song of birds was harshness to his ear,
And every gem of joy was sorrow's tear;
The hum of bees was sadness, and the leaf
Rustled but to the melody of grief.
All things the heart could feel, the eye could see,
Mirrored for him his soul's deep agony;
More deep than human hearts can ever know,
That hath not known a lover's grief and woe,
Or, felt the torture of the flames that burn
While longing to, and yet, will not return,
Because of pride, the haughty sentinel,
Whose mischief once turned heaven into hell,
If strictly true this be, not holy writ,
It dragged the angels down to people it.

Pride is a prickly bush on which there grows
A thousand thorns to one pale stunted rose;
If this you'd pluck, the chances are you'd fall,
When it you've grasped, lo, find no rose at all,
But faded leaves at last, as you draw near
All odorless, at best a painted sneer.

So Edgar found, when angered with his love,
There rose within his bosom thorns which prove
Sharper than all the thorns that ever grew
Upon the rose or thistle, and he knew
Cupid a valiant knight who would not run,
But with fierce vengeance fight when trod upon.
Rendering life a desert, waste and bare,
With sky o'ercast with clouds of black despair,
From out whose bosom sounds of discord rose
And chilling breath of terror fiercely blows,
Driving all thoughts of peace from out the breast,
Denying to the soul its cry for rest.
Bright visions of the past he oft would see,
That live, alas, alone in memory;
Will ever live, so fresh, and bright, and green,
A sad reminder of what might have been.

Thus tortured, poor Edgar pressed restlessly on
From morning till evening, from evening till dawn,
'Til nearing a river whose bright waters free
Flowed eagerly onward, to join the great sea;
When rosy-lipped morning, with soft footsteps stealing,
Came on from the eastward in glory again,
The wonderful beauty and freshness revealing
Of earth to the sight of the children of men.
Thus Edgar beheld Shiloh's valleys and hills,
The fairest the gods to the earth ever gave;
Like pure molten silver her murmuring rills
Flashed back to the sun a bright smile from each wave.
Like a bridal veil shining, the shimmering mist
Floated back from her features when morning first kissed,
With ruby lips tender, her beautiful face,
Revealing the splendor, the ease, and the grace
Of her beautiful form, in queenly robes dressed,

Bejeweled with diamonds all over her breast,
Which glittered and sparkled as though every one
Were a miniature day-god thrown off by the sun.

Bedecked with bright flowers, deep crimson, and white,
While some had unfolded their bloom in the Night,
And catching the folds of her drapery there
Had wound it about them forever to wear.

Here Nature her features had wreathed in bright smiles,
And o'er her fair form a rich mantle had flung;
All covered with mosses, her rocky defiles
With manifold voices of sweet music rung.
The sound of her laughter in sweet cadence rose
From silver-toned brooklets, that spurning repose
On clover-decked high-lands, with silvery gleam
Flashed back the warm kiss of the sun's golden beam,
As down the bright hill-sides they leapt in their glee
To join the great waves of the swift Tennessee.

Within the deep woods, which o'ershadow her hills,
And curtain the sky from the valleys below,
A city of war all her grassy sward fills
Whose white-tented dwellings resplendently glow
'Neath rays of bright sunshine which, dancing around,
Weave dark leafy patterns all over the ground.
While orioles flitting, where deep shadows are rolled,
In cool, shady nooks, where affrighted the Night
Lay trembling with terror before the Sun's light,
Were murmurs of music and flashes of gold.

Oh fair was this city when 'neath the moon sleeping,
Whose soft silvery beams fell in quietness o'er
The hills and the valleys, and river, there creeping,
As softly it sang to the camp on the shore;
While out from the sky in their wantonness roaming
The shadowy breezes with bated breath steal
The soul of the flowers, in the hours of the gloaming,
And, unto the sense, all their odors reveal.
Then laving their wings on the breast of the river,
They gather the pearls which float glittering there,
Then mounting o'er meadows and woodlands they quiver,
And scatter the gems o'er the sleeping world there !

The velvety mantle of grasses which cover
The slumbering hills, all bediamonded lay
As a sweet blushing maid, attired for her lover
To smile on her charms, so they wait for the day.

From loyal homes parting, here quickly assembled
The flower of the nation, the bravest and best,
Before whose achievements the modern world trembled,
The strength of the nation, the pride of the West.
Impatiently waiting commands for a season
To march to the battle, the soldier's delight,
To throttle the victims of error and treason,
And triumph the flag, and the cause of the right.
With the loyal and brave, the strength of the nation,
Young Edgar commingled regretting delays,
That fretted ambition, while war's preparation
Consumed the bright hours of the long Spring-time days.

Meanwhile Arzelia, lovely flower,
Bereft of reason and of power,
By cruel words which, like a dart,
Pierced through her bosom to her heart,
When told that Edgar's oath had bound
His soul to brave wild war's dread sound.
And in the heat of battle be
A mark for vengeance of the foe,
As through the conflict's bloody sea
He leads where duty calls to go.
Benumbed she lay till sorrow's tears
Came to her stricken soul's relief,
And all her trembling hopes and fears
Gave way before a flood of grief.
"Oh, love," she cried, "come back again,
Come back and still this bitter pain,
Those harsh and cruel words I said
Were false as human tongue could tell;
Oh come and lift this weight of dread,
And whisper one fond, loved farewell."

"Oh, love, am I by thee forsaken?
Oh, love, return and tell me true,
If love, sweet love, will not awaken

And bind again our hearts anew?
Oh, can it be the golden bowl,
By my rash action has been broken?
The precious life-wine of the soul
Been chilled by words that I have spoken?
Will nevermore thy joyous tone
Call me again thy heart, thine own?
And am I doomed fore'er to miss
The thrilling gladness of thy kiss?
And never feel thy hand again
Brush back the ringlets from my brow?
Shall Sorrow sit fore'er with pain
Upon my heart as she doth now?
Has peace forever flown away —
Will ne'er return love's gladsome morn?
Must I fore'er in sadness stray,
Cursing the day when I was born?
Oh, love, return and roll the stone,
Away from this dread sepulcher;
'Tis thy loved hand, and thine alone,
This precious boon can now confer."

Thus o'er and o'er she sobbed in vain,
Shrouded within her bitter woe,
Feeling remorse and constant pain,
Which hearts like hers alone can know.
The hours seemed days, and days seemed years,
While poured her heart its flood of tears,
As through her bosom swept wild fears
Lest he, her love, her soul, her life,
Should fall a victim 'mid the strife,
And she not know, this side of Heaven,
She was by him, at least, forgiven.
At thought her future life might be
Clouded by this great misery,
She vowed that she would never rest
Till by his smile she had been blessed;
Till every care had been beguiled,
And they be fully reconciled.

Upon this mission quick away
She hastened ere the close of day;

And on, still on, her course pursued,
By holy power of love imbued;
And as the Sabbath sweetly rose
She knew its radiant light would close,
And evening's gloaming shadows fall
Upon a tented city, where
Edgar would answer to her call,
And lift this weight of deep despair;
Dark waves should calm to quiet bliss,
At touch of his warm, fervent kiss.
But hark, why trembles thus the air?
Why quivers thus the solid ground?
No clouds of storm are gathered there
From which to voice this rumbling sound.
Still yet again it clearer grows,
Breaking the Sabbath's still repose.
Beneath the pleasant Spring-time sun,
It is the battle's thunder gun!
Whose tones now echo through the sky
Their challenge to all who defy,
The measure of their iron will;
With awe-inspiring tremors fill
The breasts of those who hear the sound,
While breath of vengeance all around
Beclouds the balmy Spring-time air,
With deep forebodings of despair.

"Oh, God," she murmured, "save from harm,
Amid the hurtling battle's storm;
Outstretch for him Thy mighty arm
To guard and guide his noble form."
And every breath was one of prayer
To Heaven, to save her hero there.
Surely, if prayer availing prove,
Heaven will lend an ear to her,
Inspired by holy thoughts of love
From such a fair petitioner.

The lull of battle came when Night
Drew o'er the field her somber shade,
Hiding from mortal eyes the sight
And havoc, which wild war had made

And when the twilight's softened ray
Weaves, with its strands of gloom and gray,
The bridge o'er which our senses pass,
Unless our willfulness, alas!
The ropes destroy, with ruthless hand,
Which lead to sleep's weird mystic land,
Arzelia on her mission came,
Asking, alone in love's sweet name,
That she might search that dark field o'er,
From where the river laves its shore,
Back to the farthest picket line,
Where rebel forces still combine,
To find her lover, though the field
Should naught but his dead body yield.

When the gloom of night had fallen over all the battle-field,
Where the weary armies rested from the fight, they would not yield,
But, drawn up in line of battle, waiting for the coming day,
Through that stormy night of terror, resting on their arms, they lay;
And the moaning of the wounded, as they writhed in bitter pain,
Mingled with the dreary sobbing of the fitful gusts of rain;
And each moment souls were winning over death sweet victory,
On the bloody field of Shiloh, where flows swift the Tennessee.

Wildly now the rain is falling from the sympathetic clouds,
Washing softly the dead faces lying in their loyal shrouds,
And the night winds, weirdly moaning, kiss the temples of the dead,
Chanting then a requiem sadly in the hemlocks overhead.
And the river's waves are muffled, as they softly onward sweep,
While the trees of all the forest sadly wring their hands and weep
For the fate of all those lying 'neath their branches silently,
On the bloody field of Shiloh, where flows swift the Tennessee.

For the woods were full of sadness, dead and dying, everywhere,
And the woundeds' piteous pleading floated out upon the air,
With deep, piercing tones of anguish, causing hearts to melt and quail,
That had never known a tremor, as they faced the deadly hail
In the carnival of battle, where death raged amid the storm,
And upon its dashing billows rode in many a dreadful form;
Oh, it was a scene most fearful for the human eye to see,
On the bloody field of Shiloh, where flows swift the Tennessee!

Some were praying, in their anguish, for the hand of death to free
Them from state where now they languish, in their awful misery;
Some were calling "father," "mother," in delirium of pain,
To relieve them from the torture which now fires their fevered brain
While others sang of conquest, strong in faith for victory,
Over all the foes that cherish aught against full liberty,
As they fought the battle over, struggling still in death to free
Our loved country from foul treason, where flows swift the Tennessee.

Here amid this scene of terror, with soft footsteps, gently came
Woman, with her tender kindness, in love's sweet and holy name,
Bearing Heaven's great commission to those faint and dying men;
And through all her acts and blessings, Christ, the Holy, lived again.
And the dying soldiers blest them, called them angels all divine;
And if Heaven's be their equals, how its fields must glow and shine,
For their presence was all beauty, all delight and sympathy,
As they blest the scene of battle, where flows swift the Tennessee.

'Mid the strife and rage of battle, lo! fair liberty was born,
Through deep woe, and grief, and anguish, till the evening from the morn,
'Mid the groaning, and the moaning, and the sobbing, and the pain,
While the blood from human fountains flowed, like storms of splashing rain;
And each loyal drop there falling was of more than finite worth,
For 'twas shed for Freedom's triumph, and for Liberty's great birth;
That man's brotherhood forever should be known from sea to sea—
Thus spoke forth the voice of battle, where flows swift the Tennessee.

All of honor, all of merit, that poor human power can give,
Is due all those that perished, is due all those that live,
Who here strove, and fought like heroes, 'mid the awful din and strife,
In the Nation's hour of peril, when throbbed low its pulse of life,
When the fearful scourge of treason damned and poisoned every pore,
And the light of its fair vision seemed fast dimming, more and more:
Honor, glory, fame undying, aye, forever let it be
For all those who fought for freedom, where flows swift the Tennessee.

Gather lilies from the valley, from the hillside pluck the rose,
Weave them into lovely garlands, for all those who here repose;
Bring them yearly in their freshness, for the heroes, one and all,
Whom the hand of Death here shadowed, with its dark and mystic pall.
Jewel them with pearly tear-drops, richest gifts the heart may know,
Weave them gently o'er the green mounds, for the sleepers just below,
And may angels o'er them hover, till they wake again and see
The full glory of their labors, where flows swift the Tennessee.

Arzelia, in this dreadful hour
Threaded her way across the field,
All woman's grace and human power,
Her purpose firm, she would not yield,
But back and forth amid the rain,
Hearing the agony of pain,
As, all around her, everywhere,
It rose upon the humid air
In awful sounds of dire distress,
From writhing forms whose wretchedness
The king of terrors could not swell;
Though all the flames of fiery hell
Were added to their torture there,
It could not fill the blackened air
With one more sound of wild despair.
Yet through it all, amid the storm,
Was seen to pass her angel form,
Unmindful of the bursting shell
Which tore the raven sky and fell,
Proving full oft the final doom
Which lit brave hearts into their tomb,
As from the gun-boats on the river,
Sweeping across the darkened wood,
They burst, and giant oaks would shiver,
Spilling anew life's crimson blood;
And, answering oft, the thunder-gun,
From tempest's battlements on high;
The forked lightning swift would run
Across the storm-beclouded sky;
The terror-stricken air around
And earth would tremble, at the sound.

Yet tireless, ever on and on,
As when at first her task begun,
She plied her way with searching eye,
And would earth's terrors all defy,
And risk of losing Heaven run;
For all the joys of Paradise
Were then as nothing, to her eyes,
Compared to him, her chosen one.
Now o'er a form she stumbling fell,
And heard him lisp a last "farewell;"

Another, but the angel Death
Had called before, and from him breath
Had long departed, and the eyes,
Gazing into the stormy skies,
No answering gleam of sight there gave,
Save the determined look which brave
Men carry to their final rest,
Within kind Nature's silent breast.

She softly pressed his eyelids down,
And crossed his cold and clammy hands,
Murmuring low: "The golden crown
And wreath are his in brighter lands."
Brushing the locks from off his brow
She planted there a tender kiss,
And said: "Rest well, brave stranger, now
Thy home is brighter far than this."
While sorrow's tear-drops coursing run
From out her soulful, tender eyes
At thought that every single one
Was some heart's idol, who here lies
And suffers all the heart may know
Of pain and anguish here below,
With none to sooth their agonies.

On, on she goes, still searching on,
Asking of each and every one,
Who o'er that field now swiftly move,
If they have seen her chosen love—
A noble soldier, one whose eye
Would all the hosts of earth defy;
A leader of the brave, of those
Who bid defiance to their foes,
And would that every foot of ground
Were heaped into a gentle mound,
Beneath which loyal sons should lie,
Rather than treason should defy,
And trail the white and crimson bars,
And dim the glory of the stars
Which form the banner of the free,
The Nation's badge of liberty.

But of her love no one could tell,
Save that he fought so brave and well
That his inspiring, flashing eye
Nerved all his men for victory;
That in the thickest of the fight
To lead them on was his delight,
Telling to each and every one,
No crown was like to duty done
Where honor calls, though dangers lie
As thick as sun-beams in the sky,
Or, forest's leaves, when summer's fled,
And earth by them is carpeted.

The fairest flowers are first to die —
The dearest treasures soonest lost;
The stunted oaks all storms defy,
The stately trees are wrecked and tossed;
The birds that sweetest, softest sing,
Are first to plume the farewell wing;
The voice that wakes love's sweetest tone,
Death seems to claim first for its own.

Arzelia felt these sayings true;
For all through life the hand of fate
Seemed prone to wreck and desolate
All hopes and plans she ever knew.
And now she looked alone to see
Her lover's form before her lying,
And felt her lot was sure to be
To find him wounded, weak and dying.
And when the sword of heaven, flashing,
Drove back the darkness where she stood
Amid the pelting rain, which dashing
Fell in great torrents through the wood,
As fierce the storm-king's voice awoke
The stillness of the night around,
She shelter took beneath an oak,
There saw her lover on the ground —
Just where amid the charge he fell
When near him burst a deadly shell,
Bereaving him of all but life,
While onward rolled the dreadful strife.

She bowed in grief her queenly head,
While coursing from her lovely eyes
The scalding tears of grief were shed.
'Mid choking sobs, "Alas!" she cries,
As clasping there his dear, loved form
She finds his manly bosom warm:
"Oh love, forgive, forgive, dear heart,
The words which long have kept apart
Our hungry souls; forgive, forgive,
Forgive me, love;" the bitter cry
Rang on the air, "or let me die!"
And o'er and o'er she kissed him there
On brow, and cheeks, and lips, and hair,
As with affection's fond caress
She'd woo him back to consciousness.
And so it was: now, trembling, rise
The fallen curtains of his eyes,
And from them fondly, sweetly beams
Affection's pure, devoted gleams.
Oh, power of love! Oh, matchless power!
To fill with light this gloomy hour;
To win back from the jaws of death
The soul that seemed devoid of breath.
She caught that sweet, reviving glow;
Her tears of praise in torrents flow;
In wild delirium of joy
She cries: "Thank God! my darling boy,
Thou hast returned again to me
From verge of death's deep mystery.
Oh, love, while yet thou truly live,
Speak, speak one word, that word—forgive!"

She bowed to listen, placed her ear
Close to his lips, that she might hear
The faintest accent that might wake
To voice the stillness so profound,
The longings of her soul to break,
And fill her heart with love's sweet sound.
His features beamed with radiant glow,
With beauty rare, which none may know
On earth below or heaven above,
Except it beam from souls that love.

Pressing her hand within his own,
He murmured in a pleading tone:
"Arzelia, through the awful storm
Of battle, where I fiercely rode,
I saw before me thy loved form,
There, where the fires most hotly glowed,
And war's fierce notes in discord rose,
And man to man with deadly blows
Sought to dispel, destroy, deface
The pride and blossom of the race;
With all the damned device of war
Each sought to prove proud conqueror.
But in that vision's lovely face
There seemed to hover still a frown;
What cared I then for victor's crown,
When I no sign of hope could trace
Of sweet forgiveness there to bless?
Then turned my soul to bitterness.
I curses hurled upon my fate,
That she should let all honors fall,
Save one, and that were more than all,
Without which life is desolate;
Then prayed I with each fleeting breath,
That I sweet peace might find in death;
The volley's flame was beauty then,
The cannon's roar was music sweet;
And on I urged my valiant men,
Craving not victory or defeat,
But that I might amid the fray
Wrestle with death's grim skeleton,
And close my book of life this day,
And with distress for e'er have done.
What should I care for victory,
The plaudits of the world to me
Would sound like hollow mockery,
For earth below and heaven above,
Hold not one charm without thy love.

"But, oh, Arzelia, love, with thee
Earth's bitterness to me is sweet,
And cloudless skies smile on a sea
Where fresh winds whisper lovingly,

From shores where bloom love's flowers complete;
And I would give my chance of Heaven
To live and be by thee forgiven,
And know that I was dear to thee,
As thou, sweet love, art unto me."

"Press close to me, darling, I feel the fresh breezes
From over death's ocean are kissing my brow,
Exultingly trembles my soul as it seizes
The strength, which they bring me, in ecstasy now.
I hear the sweet music of bugles so faintly
Borne over the white-crested foam of each wave,
And see in great columns my comrades all saintly
In triumph march on, over death and the grave.

"The great army of souls that now are ascending
From out this dark wood, are the souls of the brave,
The notes of the fife, with the drum's music blending,
Cheer all who have struggled their country to save.
Their robes are as pure as the light of the morning,
As over the earth its white pinions are spread,
If the world only knew, the sound of its mourning
Would change into joy for the life of the dead.

"The blood of the patriot shed in defending
The cause of sweet Liberty's triumph and right,
A plea for full pardon each soul is attending
That rises to God from this dark field to-night.
For he who hath wrought for the honor and glory
Of Him who rules over the cause of the just,
By writing in blood from his heart the sweet story
Of freedom for man, need no judgment distrust.

"My bow is unbended, and empty my quiver,
My armor falls powerless with this mortal life,
For beyond the bright waves of death's gleaming river
We wear not the armor of envy and strife.
For peace, like an angel with fair bosom heaving,
Smiles sweetly o'er all on the shores of the blest;
There sorrow is past, and all sadness and grieving,
Are lulled to a quiet and unending rest.

"Arzelia, oh, my thoughts grow tender,
And anguish fills my bleeding heart
That I, thy chosen love, defender,
Must leave thee all as lone thou art;
Heaven is sweet, I've caught its glimmer,
But, oh! to be fore'er with thee,
This world, or even one far dimmer,
Were good enough, sweet love, for me.
But now He calls, the great commander,
From the head-quarters of the soul,
And I must go, dear love, to render
Account to Him who has control
Of all the bond, and of the free,
Of this, and every other land,
Shaping their life and destiny,
By guidance of His mighty hand;
And as He wills, 'tis well it be,
He knows alone—eternity.
But, love, no mortal words can tell
How much I love thee, and how well;
How every thought, and every breath,
Has been—shall be all thine till death.
And were one thought within this heart
Unkind to thee, it should depart,
For love of thee is life alone,
Thy beaming glance, thy tender tone,
Are sweetest treasures unto me,
And shall, through all eternity,
My solace and sweet comfort be.

"Come closer, darling, I grow chill,
Strange tremors all my being fill—
And fainter grows my every breath!
Is this, oh love, can this be death?
Kiss me, and but a little weep
That I have fallen in the sleep
That ne'er shall know a mortal morn;
That to my ears no more be borne
The notes of war, while years increase,
But all be one unbroken peace,
One endless night of sweet repose,

On which no sun hath ever rose.
For me, I trust, it shall be so,
Unless thy love, I there shall know!

"Oh, dreadful thought! to think that we
Shall live no more — eternity
Be one vast, voiceless sepulcher,
To which all love and light defer!
No, no! hope shines beyond, above —
Love proves itself immortal love.
Something within all bosoms lie
Which speaks of immortality.
I feel, dear love, it must be true,
While on my brow death's clammy dew
Dims every sense of sight and sound,
And glimmers fill all space around.
Save thy angelic smile to bless
My soul with its sweet loveliness;
While brightly from the farther shore
God's light, in radiant love-beams, pour
Across death's waters, through the night
In one effulgent path of light.
I hear the splashing of the oar —
I'll soon be with thee, love, no more.
They'll call you soon, dear one, and I
Will come to waft you to the sky.
I would that I could longer dwell —"
He ceased to speak and smiled — farewell!

And with that smile his soul took wing
For brighter fields of endless light,
There in sweet peace to endless sing
Beyond the shadows of the night.
So softly was its going there,
From mortal home so true and fair,
That not a trace of pain was left
Upon his form, of life bereft,
That she was loath o'er him to weep,
Death was so like its brother — sleep.
So calm and peaceful there he lay,
While slowly wore the night away,
That she was hopeful that when morn

Should in the East again declare
That to the earth a day was born,
And waken all the sleepers there,
He, too, would waken from his dream,
And, with the old light in his eyes,
More beautiful than Spring-time skies
Unto her soul, would softly beam,
With all the sweetness of the love
Which caused so oft her heart to move
In unison, with every glance,
And all her being thrill, entrance;
And know the sweet, ecstatic bliss
Again of his warm, fervent kiss.

And in her sorrow and her tears,
There came the thought of other years,
When first upon the Nation's sky
Appeared the dark cloud of its sin,
Until it grew, till every eye
Discerned that judgment would begin
Full soon, for lo! the cloud had spread
Till all was darkness overhead,
And sullen sound of discord rose,
And forked tongues of fiery flame,
The venom of the clouds disclose,
And treason dare pronounce its name
In places high of public trust,
And flash its gleaming sword of hate,
Rendering all most desolate,
By those whose nurture had been drawn
Like babes from out the mother's breast,
Who, watching o'er them when the dawn
Of life had come at their bequest.

And when the rumbling of the storm
Had shook the Nation's peaceful form,
And she had called upon her sons
In her defence to grasp their guns,
He shook with indignation's thrill,
And answered with a loyal will.
And she remembered sadly now
The cloud which hovered o'er his brow,

As if a warning voice he heard,
Silent, yet clear, as though the word
Had been by mortal lips expressed,
And he the warning thought confessed
As, turning to her, he had said : —

"When I am dead,
Come to me then as now,
And gently soothe my brow,
And rest your hand,
Dear, loving hand,
Upon my head,
And say: 'He sleeps,
He is not dead;'
And lay your head
Upon my breast.
Think me not dead,
Only at rest.
Look on my form and face
As my last resting place,
From whence I'm fled
To house not made with hands,
In brighter, better lands,
Where soul-faith saith
There is no death."

"Oh precious thought," she softly said,
"He does but sleep, he is not dead.
This precious form of lifeless clay,
Which soon the grave shall hide away,
Is but the mansion wherein he
Was prisoned of his liberty."

Death truly is the golden key
That sets the soul at liberty,
And solves the mystery profound
To all by mortal senses bound.
This hope assuaged her grief at length,
And, like rich wine, gave to her strength,
Until her soul, on faith's strong wing,
Arose till she could firmly fling
Away all doubt, and truly say:

"He wakens to a brighter day,
To which this world's most radiant light
Is but a sad and gloomy night.

"But oh, dear form, sweet face, bright hair,
I love each line of beauty there;
Those precious lips, that oft have told
The tale of love—beside which gold
Nor all the world, nor heav'n can hold
One single thing of any worth;
From earliest hour of life's sweet birth
Until its close—could all things be,
Of beauty, light and melody,
Rolled into one, it could not prove
An equal to one word of love.

"Sweet lips, now cold and motionless,
That answer not my fervent kiss,
And ears that harken not the sound,
Though oft I break the stillness round,
With pleadings to thy noble soul;
Oh, would that death would swiftly roll
From mine this mantle dark of clay,
And show my soul to thine the way.
Dear eyes, now closed and lusterless,
Your waking light — how I shall miss!
Oh, that the lamp of life might be
But for a moment lighted there,
That I again through them might see
The soul-light beaming warm and fair,
As in the old, sweet time, when shone
Their loving light into my own.

"Oh, locks of jet and silken hair,
Clustering round that marble brow,
Thy wealth of darkened ringlets now
Circles a manly beauty rare."
To every one who passed that way,
She bade them softly, lightly move,
Lest their rude treading should betray
Their presence to her sleeping love,
And wake him from his peaceful rest,
As he so calmly, sweetly lay

With his fair head upon her breast,
While broke the darkness into day.
It would have touched a heart of stone,
To see her guard with loving care
Her precious love there all alone;
And softly kiss his brow and hair,
And murmur to him sweet and low,
As from her lips these accents flow: —

"Sweetly sleep, my darling lover,
Calmly take thy needed rest;
Angels o'er thy bosom hover,
Thou art pillowed on my breast.

"Sweetly sleep, no need of waking,
Now all care has from thee flown;
No rude call thy rest is breaking,
I am with thee, all alone.

"I will guard thee, love, forever,
It is now my chosen part;
Naught on earth can more us sever,
Hand in hand, and heart to heart.

"I am with thee, ever with thee,
Sorrow's waves have ceased to roll;
And no trouble can distress me,
I am with thee, oh! my soul.

"Heaven's richest, sweetest blessings
Crown our lives with purest joy;
With its warm and loved caressings,
I am with thee, darling boy.

"I am with thee, oh, my lover,
Earth can add no sweeter bliss;
With my mantle thee I cover
In thy slumbers thee I kiss.

"To my bosom now I fold thee,
And thy lips in fondness kiss;
In affection's arms I hold thee—
Heaven's joys exceed not this."

Thus the waking morning found her, talking softly to her dead,
While the matin winds were sighing in the branches overhead;
And rich, brilliant pearls and rubies, stud the leaves and all the ground,
As though angels in their winging, scattered here their jewels round;
And she softly said unto him, "Sleep, my lover, sleep away,
Take thy rest, oh, take thy slumber, heed thou not the coming day.

"Heed thou not the cannon's thunder, heed thou not the voice of war,
Though the vase of clay be broken, yet the soul is conqueror."
Still I seem to hear her singing, to her lover, soft and low:
"Sleep, my darling, take thy slumber, thou no care shalt ever know;
For I'm with thee, ever with thee, sorrow's waves hath ceased to roll,
And no troubles can distress thee, I am with thee, oh, my soul.

"Where thou leadest, I will follow,
Where thou goest, I will go;
Thou, my god, my fair Appollo;
Other's love I shall not know.

"Queen to thee, my lord and master,
Glowing with pure love divine,
Through the scenes of wild disaster,
Strong my heart with love's sweet wine.

"I shall follow, dear Appollo,
Though thy path should lead through flame;
Other joys are bitter—hollow,
To the sweetness of thy name.

"Thou wilt waken, and say to me
With thy lips, and soulful eyes:
'Love, my bosom calls unto thee,
As the sea calls to the skies.'"

And o'er and o'er his lips she kissed,
'Mid that weird scene where on the mist
Of early morning softly lay,
Wooed unto pulsing waves of gray,
By rosy wings of waking day.

Still he dreamed on when morn returned,
And gave no sign of waking there,
Though long the maiden watched and yearned,
And softly stroked his raven hair.
The horologe of time marked not
For him the hour, and morn forgot
To wake him from his peaceful dreams,
Though full she threw her golden beams
Upon his peaceful face and brow,
Wreathed in a smile of beauty now.

Sleep gently pressed his eyelids down,
Burnished with light his raven crown;
Mother of dreams, oh! gift divine!
Wine of the gods! refreshing wine!
Renewing life and giving power,
And peace to all; welcome the hour
When thou dost bid us cease to weep,
Angel of mercy — peaceful sleep.
"Brother of Death!" if so thou be,
Death holdeth naught of misery,
As softly o'er our senses creep,
Thy calm, unconscious reign.
We welcome thee, oh, gentle sleep,
And woo thee oft to come again;
A balm for every sorrow thou,
A priceless crown for every brow;
Proving His matchless love so deep,
"He giveth His beloved sleep."

As closed her low, sweet lullaby,
Her sorrow woke with heaving sigh;
As back with mortal sense again,
She felt the burden of her pain
Fall on her heart with sore distress,
Making her grief nigh measureless;
Her troubled soul all bliss denied,
In agony of woe she cried: —
"Oh, how I loved him, none can tell,
I cannot, will not, say farewell!
I cannot live without him, no—

'Where'er thou goest, I will go,'
Are words which ne'er can be unsaid,
They bind the living and the dead;
For none are dead, they live to-day,
Though in a higher, purer way;
Those solemn words I shall obey,
And from this spot I shall not move
Till Heaven take me to my love."

Then, lo, from out the mystic gloaming,
From the land of spirits roaming,
Came a presence hovering o'er her,
In the form of her dead lover,
Speaking with voice that was his own
In every accent, every tone;
In every feature of its face
A like to his she there could trace;
The eyes — those wondrous pleading eyes,
Glancing from out the darkened skies,
With all the wealth of tenderness
Embodied in the soul of love,
Voicing the power supreme to bless,
Known to the earth or heaven above,
And, whispering to her soul, it said:—
"Arzelia, love, I am not dead,
But from the prison-house of clay
I, that you loved, have passed away;
Oh, precious one, be of good cheer,
The hour of joy for you is near,
E'en now death's waters lave your feet,
A little time and we shall meet —
Oh, blessed thought, to part no more!
Upon this radiant, love-kissed shore.
Thou wert by nature made so near
This better world, your change will be
Without a tremor or a fear,
From earth to immortality,
And peacefully as doth the rose
Its blossom from the bud disclose.
Here, where no joy is e'er denied,
And every wish is satisfied;

Where wakes no thought within the breast
That findeth not a peaceful rest.
Wherever sent, the searching dove
Returns with joyful news of love.
Where every questioning echo dies,
Amid the sound of glad replies,
Within these fields of Paradise.

"Take all the glory of the stars
From shimmering mist to sun-like Mars,
Add silvery glimmer of the moon,
And golden beams of sun at noon;
The soulful murmur of the seas,
The lute-like notes of woodland breeze,
The freshness of all winds that blow,
The sweetness of all flowers that bloom,
And every joy that's found below,
Between the cradle and the tomb,
And roll them into one grand ball
Of love and beauty, light and song,
And into heaven let it fall
Amid the soul-redeeméd throng,
And it would all far lesser be
Than morning dew-drop to the sea."
Then, beckoning her with smile and hand,
The vision slowly passed away,
While from the eastward o'er the land,
Faint glimmers hinted of the day.

Oh, cruel grief, how worse than leaden ball,
Thy course to loving heart, withering all
The budding beauty of the maiden life,
When trembles all the soul at thought of wife;
Of wife to him of her pure bosom's choice,
When love awakens with his lute-like voice,
And all the seasons bear the breath of June,
And every waking sound melts to a tune;
And life appears all rose without the thorn,
And night gives way to one effulgent morn
Of light and joy, whose bright and golden ray,

Bespeaks till death one endless Summer day.
Oh, cruel grief, why should the fates let fall
Thy bitterness, to damn and wither all;
Why should the Winter winds untimely blow,
And fill the warm-lipped month of June with snow,
With thy dread kiss of death to blast the rose,
Destroy the sweetness of its fragrant bloom,
Strip life of every joy, and but disclose
The weird and ghastly terror of the tomb?

Oh, blasting grief, before thee light is fled,
And hope's sweet face is mantled with a pall:
For he, the fountain of her joy, is dead,
Has passed the Rubicon of life beyond recall;
And she is widowed and bereft — alone,
With her great weight of sorrow only known
Unto her soul, and Him that feeds the lambs,
And to the hungry heart doth give rich alms;
But in this wretched world of black despair,
How madly hurls the Winter through the air,
And freezing the young life in every pore,
And deafening all with its wild, frantic roar,
As high the billows rage of sorrow's storm,
Till cowering 'neath its blast her gentle form
Trembles beneath her heavy weight of grief,
As shakes, before the howling winds, the leaf;
Benumbed with grief, the night hours pass away,
And in the East appears the blush of day,
And as the infant morn trembled with life,
She woke to sorrow's pain, which like a knife,
Struck to her soul, when morning light had said,
With truthful ray, "poor heart, thy love is dead."
She answered with one wild and piercing scream,
Which echoed through the wood and down the stream,
So full of human agony and pain,
Its like shall never sound on earth again.
And fell there in the morning's twilight hour,
A crushed and broken lily — love's sweet flower,
Divorced on earth, but wedded now in Heaven,
Unto the soul her love on earth was given.

And there, upon a mossy bed,
They found them lying cold and dead;
He died his country's life to save,
And blessed by all shall be his grave.
While the soft wind said to the leaf,
"Poor troubled heart, she died of grief!"
And sweeping low to kiss them there,
Lying within death's mystic fold,
It toyed and tossed their brilliant hair
In waves of mingled jet and gold.

DIALECT POEMS

UNIV. OF
CALIFORNIA

MUSIC IN THE BARKIN' UV A DOG

MUSIC IN THE BARKIN' UV A DOG.

What's the sweetest music? stranger,
  That's a question, I'll agree;
Fur to differ frum most others,
  Though there's one that sides with me.
Music's what brings joy 'nd comfort,
  Moves to pain, mayhaps to tears;
Paints a picter, clear, unfadin',
  On the heart, fur years 'nd years.
Some likes organ, some pianner,
  Flute er fiddle, some a band;
But fur me a good dog's barkin's,
  The sweetest music in the land.

You'r astonished at my choosin',
  Sich a note fur best uv all
Uv the sounds which earth or heaven,
  Ever on my ear let fall?
Listen, stranger, 'nd I'll tell you,
  How I come to take the ground,
That a dog's voice, when he's barkin',
  Makes on earth the sweetest sound:
It was evenin' in the Summer,
  We'd been married most four year;
Strange it seems in lookin' back'ard,
  How that evenin' seems so clear.

I hed finished up my chorin',
  To the milkin' uv the cows;
They wuz still down in the pastur',
  Whar they lov'd so much to browse.
Nell, our baby, lyin' yonder,
  In the corner uv the yard,
With the golden-fingered willows
  Ever o'er her keepin' guard.
Wuz ez peart a three-year baby,
  Ez ever come on earth to dwell;
But she died uv scarlet fever
  Two years after what I tell.

I hed whistled fur old Rover,
  'Nd let down the pastur' bars,
'Bout the time the daylight faded,
  'Nd the angels lit the stars.
I could hear the bell a-clinkin',
  Like ez if old Pied wuz still,
Nippin' uv the grass a-growin'
  'Neath the elms by the mill.
Rover after 'em went skippin',
  At a gestur' uv my hand,
'Nd wuz soon a-drivin' homeward
  Every critter in the band.

Tinkle, tinkle, ling-lang, ling-lang,
  Coming home et milkin' time;
Wuz the chune the bell wuz playin'
  A reg'lar milk 'nd butter chime.
On they come, the dog a-drivin'
  Uv 'em thro' the pastur' lot,
Pied the forid rank a-leadin',
  Follered clost by Red 'nd Spot.
Then the heifers — playful critters,
  Come a-tossin' uv their heads,
But soon settled, like most youngsters
  After supper, to their beds.

I wuz finishin' the milkin'
  Uv the little brindle cow,
Which wuz jest the boss of "creamers;"
  Spot guv more milk, I'll allow,
But twant half so good fur butter,
  'Nd our little baby Nell
Wouldn't drink uv nary other;
  Couldn't fool 'er — she could tell
Brindle's milk frum all the others,
  'Nd her "tup" would alluz bring;
'Nd I'd milk et full uv "strippins,"
  Coz et pleased the little thing.

Ez I finished up that evenin',
  'Nd turn'd round to take her cup,
Found she wuzn't no whar near me,
  'Nd I went to hunt her up;
Went out whar I see her standin',
  When I got the pail 'nd stool,
Ez I started in to milkin',
  Whar she waited ez a rule.
But she want no whar in hearin',
  Fur I called her loud 'nd long;
But no answer come back to me,
  Save the wind now blowin' strong.

Then I listened; called 'nd listened,
  But the moanin' uv the trees
Wuz the only sound I gathered
  Frum the wingin' uv the breeze.
"Come in, John, 'nd bring the baby!"
  Called out Mary from the door;
"Don't you see a storm is brewin'?
  Can't you hear the thunder roar?"
"Yes," I answered, "I am comin',"
  'Nd I rushed about half wild;
Huntin' every nook 'nd corner,
  Fur our darlin' little child.

On the storm-cloud come a-rushin',
  Makin' things ez black ez night;
'Nd I knew she wuzn't near me,
  Fur the child war dressed in white.
Then I heard old Rover barkin',
  Way off in the pastur' wood;
'Nd I know'd he'd find the baby,
  Quicker'n any human could.
So I called, 'nd called, 'nd whistled,
  But old Rover wouldn't come;
'Nd I felt I'd like to kill 'im,
  Strange ez how I wuz so dumb.

Then I rushed down in the pastur',
  Heerd 'im barkin' more 'nd more;
Followed down whar the black waters,
  O'er the mill dam foamin' pour.
I hed come quite close up to 'im,
  'Fore I see thar on the ground,
Little Nell, who wuz a-cryin',
  But, thank God, all safe 'nd sound.
I hev heard all kinds uv music,
  Mentioned in the catalogue;
But since then, there's none that's sweeter
  Than the barkin' uv a dog.

LITTLE CRICKET.

We called 'im Little Cricket,
  He wuz ez sweet a child
Ez ever gladdened human heart,
  Er with affection smiled;
And handsome! Why, the little lad
  Hed laughin' eyes 'nd curls,
'Nd ways ez sweet 'nd winsomelike
  Ez enny little girls.
He wuz a little shaver then,
  A-borderin' on four;
The time when heaven to children gives
  All things we must adore.
The way he crept into our hearts
  And grappled every string,
And ruled us all et his sweet will,
  Wuz like a little king!
There want a man in the hull camp
  But loved 'im ez his own,
With love ez tender an' ez pure
  Ez enny ever known.

His father wuz my partner,
  'Nd ez good 'nd brave a man
Ez ever struck the hills fer gold
  With miner's pick 'nd pan.
His mother wuz a faithful wife—
  One uv those jewels pure,
Who fer the loved ones uv their heart
  Would ennything endure.
She died afore the little babe
  Her mother-love hed known,
And Tom wuz left with Cricket here
  To struggle on alone.
There want a woman in the camp,
  For then the hills wuz wild;
About the last place on the earth
  'Twuz fer a little child;
But Tom wuz mother to the babe,
  And et wuz sweet to see
The lovin', patient care he gave
  To et so tenderly.

The baby somehow grew 'nd thrived,
  Escapin' all the ills
Which like a host uv doubts 'nd fears,
  The parent bosom fills;
He wuz so peart 'nd cheerin' like
  He jest reached out 'nd drew
The feelin's uv all hearts to him,
  'Nd worked 'em through 'nd through.
When et wuz Christmas 'nd the lad
  Wuz jest a-turnin' three,
His Pa allowed thet we must have
  Fer him a Christmas tree.
The notion took like wild-fire,
  And all around about,
Yer could a-heard the miners all
  Second'd et with a shout!
Each one uv us fell to 'nd worked
  Upon this novel drift,
All bent upon discoverin'
  The finest Christmas gift.

There want no gewgaws in them parts,
  And every one wuz thrown
Upon his own resources, which
  We found not overgrown!
We owe to Nature every thing
  We get, while here we live,
But in most cases all her gifts
  Are somewhat primitive;
And most uv 'em would hardly do,
  I think we'll all agree,
Fer decoratin' fer a child
  A pleasin' Christmas tree!
There ain't a soul in all the earth
  But et would please to see
The gifts which we all worked 'nd brung
  To thet ar' child uv three;
And when we hed arranged 'em all
  Et wuz a purty sight;
Ef I should live a hundred year,
  I'd ne'er forget that night.

The tree wuz right smart uv a spruce
  Set in a cedar block,
Right in the center uv the room
  On which to hang our stock;
And when we'd hung our presents all,
  That tree hed cur'us fruit;
'Twuz wagons, 'barrows, picks 'nd spades
  And other things to boot!
One feller'd gone 'nd caught a 'coon,
  Another'd shot a fox
And made fer 'im the cutest caps
  'Nd warmest kind uv frocks;
Whistles, 'nd jumpin' jacks, 'nd drums,
  And every kind uv toy
Ez enny uv us could opine
  Would ever please the boy.
And Little Cricket laughed with glee,
  With joy a-most went mad,
'Nd every man in the hull camp
  Wuz mighty nigh ez glad.

Some months passed by, 'nd when the Spring
  The hills hed carpeted
With softest grasses green 'nd fresh,
  And poppies gold 'nd red;
Our Cricket wuz a-runnin'
  And a-playin' by the brook,
And in each corner all about
  Wuz taken uv a look;
Et jest seemed that all nature wuz
  So sweet, 'nd pure, 'nd mild,
And thet her every tone 'nd smile
  Wuz mirrored in the child.
When the wild flowers bloomed the fairest,
  And Spring-time skies wuz blue,
Ez enny thet the golden stars
  Hed ever twinkled through,
Our little treasure pined away,
  And God to us denied,
The sweetest jewel uv our lives,
  When Little Cricket died.

Et would a-broke yer heart to see
  The grief uv Cricket's Pa,
Fer while love ez sweet 'nd tender,
  Et's nature's strongest law.
I tell yer et wuz terrible
  To see his silent grief,
Ez he bowed o'er that little form,
  A-trimblin' like a leaf;
His looks wuz so appealin' like,
  And heavy came his breath,
When he fust realized the truth
  Uv little Cricket's death.
He took the cold form in his arms,
  Although he knew 'twuz clay,
And pressed et to his heart 'nd walked
  The cabin floor all day.
When evenin' came we laid the child
  Beside his Ma to rest,
A-prayin' thet his spirit form
  Wuz on her spirit breast.

The clouds wuz weepin' softly like —
  The brook 'nd every leaf
Sounded ez ef they, too, wuz touched,
  By Tom's unspoken grief.
The Summer passed, and then the Fall
  Gave way to Winter's place;
Fer every day a year wuz writ
  Upon my partner's face.
When Christmas came he got a tree,
  And brought the toys 'nd things,
And fixed 'em ez they wuz last year,
  To which his mem'ry clings.
When evenin' came he set him down
  Beneath the tree alone;
When mornin' broke, he knew it not,
  His spirit sad hed flown!
There ain't no doubt enters my mind
  But thet his soul wuz given,
To wife 'nd child he loved so well,
  For Christmas up in heaven.

EZ FAITHFUL EZ A DOG.

The yaller threads uv sunlight fell
  Acrost the rollin' plain,
Jest ez ef the cloudless skies
  Wuz weepin' golden rain;
The breezes crept among the grass,
  And shook each slender blade,
Ez ef to "tag" each one uv 'em—
  The game we children played
Way back, when we wuz little folks,
  And fooled the hours away;
Jest so the breezes seemed ter do,
  Upon this Autumn day.
My pony jogged a lazy pace
  Acrost the prairie sea,
Which 'lowed my thoughts ter amble like
  Through halls o' memory:
'Til I wuz fur and fur remov'd
  Frum every sight 'nd sound
Which lay stretched out before me,
  'Nd filled the air around.

I wandered o'er the days gone by,
  (Uv course all in my mind)
And stopped a moment at the spots
  I'd loved 'nd left behind.
The old log house where I wuz born,
  Half hid with tangled vines,
Which clum about the winders like
  'Nd took the place of blinds,
Keepin' the sun frum comin' in,
  With full force on the floor,
'Nd crept about the porch 'nd wove
  An arch-way o'er the door.
I seem'd ter smell the flowers that bloom'd
  Along the graveled walk,
'Nd hear the voices, now long dead,
  Jest as they used ter talk;
Myself a little shaver there,
  A-playin' by the stream,
A-chasin' butterflies 'nd bugs,
  'Twas like a sollum dream.

My pony sudden called me back
  By givin' sech a snort,
Ez ef he feared his roamin' days
  Wuz 'bout ter be cut short.
I brought my trusty rifle up,
  'Nd jerked my pistols round,
'Nd swept the landscape et a glance,
  Fur et was level ground.
There want no movin' thing in sight,
  Save buzzards in the sky,
Whose silent shadders circled round
  About us very nigh.
'Nd then I know'd them birds hed come
  Et call of something's death;
Thet they hed scented frum afur
  The victim's tainted breath.
My broncho wuz a-lookin' like
  All life was in his eyes,
'Nd I wuz still half guardin' gainst
  Some dangerous surprise.

EZ FAITHFUL EZ A DOG.

I seed a wavin' uv the grass,
  Which wuz not uv the wind;
Looked clost, an' seed that et wuz made
  By some four-footed kind.
A moment more 'nd then a dog
  Come slowly creepin' on;
He wuz the wust sight thet my eyes
  Hed ever fell upon.
So weak and starved, he couldn't walk,
  But slowly crawled to me,
With his great brown eyes fixed on mine,
  Pleadin' fur sympathy.
My heart ain't soft ez 't useter wuz,
  I couldn't see quite clear,
'Nd when I rubbed my eye, my hand
  Wuz moistened with a tear.
I jumped frum thet 'er broncho quick,
  'Nd kneelin' on the ground,
I took thet dog's head in my lap,
  Ez though a child I'd found.

My canteen yielded up the hull
  Uv life et hed ter give;
I'd rather die with sech a dog
  Ez with some humans live.
To see the thanks those great eyes looked,
  'Nd hur his greatful whine,
Wuz honest pay fur timely help,
  Frum Nature's richest mine.
He struggled to his feet, 'nd then
  Gazed back the way he'd come,
Looked wistful like, 'nd whined, 'nd pulled,
  'Nd said in language dumb:
"I've sumethin' hur thet needs your aid,
  Come with me, Sur, and see."
I followed on, the sight I saw
  Will die with memory:
There on the ground some white bones lay,
  Bleached by the rain and sun;
Perfect in every part wur they,
  A human skeleton!

There this grand, noble dog hed stood,
  Through snow, 'nd rain, 'nd flood;
A faithful guard uv him he loved
  Ez pure ez human could.
The grass wuz trampled all about,
  Where he hed walked his beat;
All birds 'nd beasts of prey hed met,
  Fur ghoulish hopes, defeat.
The dog, himself a skeleton,
  Most pitiful to see,
Lay down 'nd whinin' died, 'nd turn'd
  His vigil o'er to me.
I hollowed out a grave fur 'em,
  'Nd side by side I lay
The bones uv master 'nd uv dog,
  'Nd went my lonely way,
A-thinkin' what a welcome home,
  All souls would sure receive,
Ef they wuz faithful ez a dog,
  Though they no creed believe.

THE SPERIT MESSENGER.

Slowly the feathery snowflakes fell
  Down through the humid air;
A-windin' round ez ef they loved
  To kinder loiter there.
The sky wuz covered with a shroud
  Uv thick and sombre gray;
Fur ez the eye could see, the flakes,
  Wuz skippin' in their play.
The ground wuz brown 'nd bare at morn,
  But long 'fore noon 'twuz white;
The trees festooned with parian wreaths—
  They wuz a purty sight.

Et kept a-fallin' all day long,
  'Nd weavin' o'er the breast
Uv Nature a grand mantle, 'til
  She all in white wur dressed.
Talk 'bout adornin' ez a bride!
  No bride on earth below
Could ever look ez pure 'nd fair
  As that true virgin, snow.
'Nd then I don't know's 'twould be best;
  People so awful good,
I've found, have less of sympathy
  Than helpful bein's should.

I wuz a-settin' by the fire,
  After the gloamin' fell;
The storm wuz whistlin' round the eaves,
  With many a screech 'nd yell,
Ez though the very imps of hate,
  Wuz seekin' with each breath,
To freeze the marrow o' the bones
  Uv all who waited death.
I wuz rejoicin' that for me,
  The storm no terrors brought,
'Nd chucklin' o'er my comforts like,
  Perhaps, more 'an I ought.

Old Prince was lyin' on the floor,
  Within the firelight's gleam,
A-restin' like frum vexins free,
  Ez in a quiet dream.
Perhaps et wuz a dream — I've hearn
  Folks speak uv stranger things,
Ez how distress er sudden joy,
  Flies 'bout on spirit wings.
But sure ez dogs ez faithful, friend,
  I seed another come,
'Nd stand in front of Prince, right there,
  'Nd say in language dumb:

"I want your help, old fellow, 'nd
  Ef you will come with me,
I'll show you how to do some good,
  'Nd show yer sympathy."
Prince bounded up, an' out the door
  He flew a-barkin' loud;
'Fore I wuz fair awake, he wuz
  Wrapped in the fallin' shroud.
I hustled on my boots 'nd furs,
  An' followed, ez I could,
Down through the clearin', 'nd beyond
  Through the deep, heavy wood.

'Nd there I found him moanin' loud,
  'Nd callin' through the storm,
Fur me to take a traveler in,
  'Nd keep 'im safe and warm.
There o'er the master's lay the form
  Uv his true, noble friend,
Alike in life 'nd death the same:
  Faithful unto the end.
'Nd when his final breath expired,
  His soul, on spirit wing,
Went out to Prince as messenger,
  His master help ter bring.

BEAUTY ON A POINT.

Thar ez somethin' mighty catchin' in the smart 'nd silent way
Uv the bird dog in approachin' the cover uv his prey;
The way uv his discernin' whar the quail er snipe ez hid,
'Nd never bein' fooled about some other bird inste'd;
Jest watch 'im when a-stiffenin' ez every limber joint
Becomes ez rigid ez a stone, when comin' to a point.

The beautiful Llewellyn, er the pointer slick 'nd trim,
Makes a pictur' so attractin' thet et makes all others dim;
Leastwise, et seems so unto me 'nd other sportsmen, too,
And ef your eyes can see jest right, 'twill seem so unto you;
Fer Nature's done her level best, the bird dog to anoint,
With her best style uv beauty, when a-comin to a point.

OUR TONIEST SASSIETY.

Our folks's SOME folks now, you bet!
  Alluz in fer songs an' rimes;
There ain't nary other set
  Hez sech gosh, all-whoopen times.
Candy pullin's, huskin bees,
  Singin' skewls an' spellin's tew;
Look the airth o'er whar yer please,
  Beatin' us ez hard ter do.

Ours's the oldest family here,
  Settled back in forty-nine;
Pop wuz out a-shootin' deer,
  When he struck the Crœsus mine.
Laws a-me! the gold he got
  Out uv the fust "lead" he struck,
More'n filled the stewin' pot.
  'Twuz a most amazin' luck!

Then a feller cum along,
  Nicest man yer ever see;
An' the heft uv all his song
  Wuz about the mine an' me!
Sed that pop should drop the pick,
  Mam an' me should wear fine gowns,
An' be just ez nice an' slick
  Ez the ladies uv the towns.

Pop, he listened ter his talk,
  An' they made sum papers out;
'Fore long Pop he had ter "walk,"
  Can't see how et cum about.
But he's rustled long quite well,
  An' ain't nearly busted yet;
An' we're livin' still ter tell
  How ter govern uv our set.

OUR TONIEST SASSIETY.

We've the biggest house about,
  Got a dandy dancin' room;
An there ain't no sort uv doubt,
  That we'll ketch on with the "boom."
There ain't no sech folks for style,
  We're the top, my ma an' me.
Lord! et does some people rile
  'Cause we lead sassiety!

We're particklar 'bout our set,
  Only let in jest the best;
Browns's left out in the wet,
  They'r not our selectedest.
'Twouldn't do fur them 'ar gals
  Ter cum in a set with me;
Scan'lous how thar daughter Sal's
  Gittin' forred-like an' free.

She do think she be so smart,
  But the things what she don't know
'Ud break down a loggin' cart,
  For she's more'n twicest ez slow.
Last week, down ter Sunday skewl,
  She was flirtin' with her eyes,
An' allowin' Lemuel's mule,
  Wuz better'n eny uv its size.

She must think he's little sense,
  Fer ter think the likes o' her,
Be's uv any consequence,
  Fer her people never wur.
He's a right smart of a man,
  An' his mother ain't so slow;
'Lowed I looked right spick an' span,
  In my new red calico.

Lemuel's smit with me, I know,
  Though he talks with other girls;
Mirandy Jinks an' Lucy Snow—
  Seed 'im pull Mirandy's curls!
But whenever he's with me,
  He grows silent and so shy,
That he's lovin', I kin see;
  He don't do much else 'an sigh!

Cupid's sech a cur'ous elf;
  When he's shootin' uv his bow,
The hit heart hol's still, itself,
  So's ter get another blow!
Willin' game ez soonest caught,
  But again it might be rude,
An' I don't know ez I ought,
  Turn pursuer when pursued!

My red dress ez sech a fit,
  Other girls haint got no show;
'Taint no wonder Lemuel's smit
  On sech charms ez mine, yer know!
Wisht he'd hurry up a bit;
  Christmas time'll soon be here,
An' I wisht that we cud get
  Married 'fore the comin' year.

When I get 'im now you bet,
  He won't talk ter other girls;
'Bout one lesson an' he'll let
  S'm'other feller pull their curls!
Next chance that he gets ter speak,
  I'll jest help 'im all I can—
An' I'll say when he's most weak,
  "Speak up, Lemuel, be a man!"

LIVIN' FUREVER IN A DAY.

I've hearn 'em tell uv pleasures rare,
But 'talluz seem'd ter me
Az most uv folks wuz deaf an' dumb,
An' through smoked glasses see.
They'll wander round and spend ther time
Alone with folks and books,
Az ef thar want no sech good things
Az mountains, groves an' brooks.
What I can't see's why people should
Take all things second hand ;
Why not go out an' gather 'em
Fresh frum the sea an' land ?

This readin' what some feller writ,
Or listenin' to his yarn
'Bout what he sees of this 'ere world,
To me ain't wuth a darn,
I'd ruther go an' get et fresh
From Mother Nature's lips ;
The truth from her in one short hour
Will all his tales eclipse.
This lookin' through some other's eyes,
I'd most ez lief be blind ;
An' they be blind ez so's content —
Least wise thet ez my mind.

An' to all those ez think they know
  Life's object's gettin' wealth,
I want ter tell thet gold ez trash
  Compar'd to bloomin' health.
The mountain brook sings sweet fur all,
  An' nary bogus note
Wuz ever issued by the choir
  With feathers on their throat.
Ef these 'ere things yer want ter prove,
  Jest go alone ter see;
Fur whar ther's ary other one,
  Thar ain't no room fur me.

An' so I'm goin' out next week,
  Up in the mountains, whar
The foamin' waters never cease
  Thar feelin's to declar;
Whar soft winds whisper 'mong the trees,
  An' wild birds carol free,
An' chipmunks gambol all day long
  'Til sunset paints the sea.
I'll "cast" my flies in that ar stream,
  An' hook the gamy trout,
An' live furever in a day
  Afore you'v found et out.

MABEL GRAY

MABEL GRAY.

I.

IN the mountains to the westward,
    In the country's early day,
Dwelt a woodman, with his family,
    From the city far away.
Their lone cot was always cheerful
    With reward of honest toil,
Forgetting all the outer world
    With its bustle and turmoil.
Lived in peace, enjoying plenty,
    For their wants were very few,
In this wildness knew more pleasure
    Than the city ever knew.
From the mountains, to the westward
    Came a low-voiced river's flow,
Which had birth amid the mountains,
    Hooded with eternal snow.
To the southward, a short distance,
    Cradled in the wooded hills,
Lay a lake, and in its bosom
    Heaven's bright reflection dwells.
On the loftiest hill surrounding
    Grew a pine-tree on its crest,
Where a pair of war-like eagles
    For long years had built their nest.
Now the Summer was departing,
    And the Autum's sombre breath
Kissed the grass, and flowers, and foliage—
    Left them beautiful in death.

Maple leaves with gold were burnished ;
    Oak leaves dipped in Summer's blood ;
And the poplar leaves were ashen,
    Brilliant all the Autumn wood.
And the changing of the season
    Could be seen all o'er the land,
While the willow and the pine tree
    Held the dying Summer's hand.

In this beauteous spot, enchanted,
    Dwelt in love and quietness
Husband, wife, and two sweet children,
    Rivaling Eden's loveliness ;
Two sweet, gentle, lovely sisters,
    One with mother's hair and eyes,
Shaming with their wondrous beauty
    Summer's gold and mellow skies ;
While the other mirrored father's
    Eyes of brown, and her rich hair

Caught some of the twilight shadows
  And, entangling, held them there.
Fannie was the younger sister,
  Scarcely turned the age of four;
Mabel's years did her's outnumber
  By perchance a half a score,
So that she was to her sister
  Guardian, playmate, guide and friend
And her constancy undying
  Was devoted to the end.

In this Autumn's early season,
  As the angels of the morn
In the East began proclaiming
  That another day was born,
Roused the husband and the father,
  Roused the mother and the wife,
He, to start upon a journey,
  She, to warn him of the strife
And the dangers all about him,
  As his solitary way,
To the distant village, eastward,
  Through wild woods and marshes lay.
Reassuring, then, he kissed her;
  Held her fondly to his breast;
Kissed his loving children sleeping,
  Smiling sweetly in their rest.
Silently he prayed God's blessing
  Might be with them, night and morn,
And His guardian spirit guide them
  Safely, until his return.
Then he hastily departed
  Up the winding eastern way,
As the sky was growing brighter
  With the heralds of the day.
When he reached the mountain summit,
  He turned round, to view the scene
Of the valley far below him,
  Slumb'ring calmly and serene.
The river's peaceful, winding course,
  Down the mountains, through the mist,

Which, by rosy lips of morning,
    Into beauty had been kissed;
The lake glowing like the armor
    Of some knightly warrior bold,
While over all the scene was thrown
    Autumn's robe of brown and gold;
And nestling 'mid the maple trees
    His rude home, where loved ones dwell;
On them all he asks God's blessing,
    And then breathes a fond farewell.
Softly creep the rays of sunshine,
    O'er the eastern mountain's brow;
All the river and the woodland
    Glow with sunlit beauty now.

Then the mother wakes the children,
    And their frugal meal prepares,
And to gather fruits for Winter,
    To the orchard wild repairs,
Charging, first, the elder sister
    With the darling baby's care,
That no sorrow come unto her,
    Clouding childish face so fair.
Then strong-hearted, busy-fingered —
    For love made her labor light —
'Til the Gheber's god, declining,
    Hinted of the coming night ;
When, returning to her dear home,
    Rich with heavy-laden store,
Of the gifts which Nature, freely,
    Giveth ever to the poor;
Found the house all strangely silent:
    Through the careless, open door,
Streamed the evening's golden sunlight,
    O'er the rough-hewn, puncheon floor.
But no children came to greet her,
    And no welcome caught her ear.
Then her bosom quick was heaving
    With a weight of awful fear;
Searched she quickly all the house through,
    And the clearing round about ;

Came no answer to her calling,
 Save the echo of her shout.
Mad with fear, with terror stricken,
 Here and there she rushed in haste,
Calling loudly to her darlings —
 But deserted was the place.
"Speak, ye stones, ye trees, and tell me!
 Speak, oh speak, ye silent air!
Tell me, oh ye winds, in sighing,
 Where my precious children are!"
Night came on, and yet no tidings
 From her loved ones could she hear;
Silent all the scene about her,
 As of one vast sepulcher.

All night long, from out the darkness,
 Hideous forms and shapes arose,
As of damnéd spirits mocking
 At her misery and woes:
Saw them seize her darling children,
 As in wild and fiendish glee;
Dance and chatter, wildly laughing,
 At her awful misery.
Then she rose and dashed upon them —
 For all hell, with fury wild,
Cannot conquer the deep passion,
 Of a mother for her child.
This the picture — this the torture,
 O'er and o'er, and o'er again,
Like a sea of seething madness,
 Rolling on her heart and brain;
Calling God to save her darlings
 From the phantom demon's rage;
Through that night's long hours of darkness—
 Every moment was an age!
For deep sorrow checks time's motion,
 While one's life flows swiftly on,
So that ages pass ere morrow,
 Breaks the darkness with its dawn.

So it was with this poor mother:
 Every feeling of her heart

Had been strained until each life-cord
    Was full ready now to part.
Morning came, and then the neighbors,
    Hearing of the children lost,
Started out, in haste, to find them,
    Caring not for any cost.
Searched they through the fields and forests,
    Dragged the lake and river-bed,
But they yielded up no token:
    Surely, then, they were not dead!
For the river's lips, though ever
    Murmuring their low, sweet sound,
Are most treacherous and cruel,
    As the world has ever found.
Many innocent and lovely
    Ones, have found beneath its waves,
From a life of joyous sunshine,
    Sudden, dark, untimely graves.
And the lake with placid bosom,
    Seeks our fears to e'er beguile,
Yet its grasp is dreadful murder,
    And, while murdering, would smile.

"Fannie! Fannie! Come here, darling!"

II.

A LONE hunter in the forest,
In the wild and trackless waste,
Where the foot of pale-faced human
Never had before been placed,
Laid him down to rest a moment,
In that wilderness alone,
When his practiced ear was startled
By a far-off human tone.
He inclined his head to listen —
Softly, faintly on the breeze,
Came a gently murmuring cadence,
Floating weirdly through the trees.
'Twas a tone of gentle pleading,
Full of love and tenderness,

As of one whose soul was troubled,
With a load of deep distress:
"Fannie! Fannie! come here, darling!"
Were the words it seemed to say;
"We must hasten home to mother,
From this dismal place away;
Come here, Fannie, come here, darling,
Fly from sister not away,
For with searching I'm so weary,
And we must no longer stay.
Come to sister, little darling,
Come, I've found your little hood;
We must hasten home to mother,
From this dark and dismal wood."
"I was dreaming—surely dreaming,"
Said he, as he heard no more;
"It was but the soft wind's sighing,
Through the trees and o'er the moor."
Then he heard the bushes rustle;
Heard a soft and stealthy tread.
Seized he quick his trusty rifle,
With a feeling of deep dread;
For his nerves were badly shaken
With the weirdness of the sound;
Could it be that this wild forest
Was enchanted, haunted ground?
Like a statue stood he, fearing
To breathe freely, lest his breath
Should give warning of his presence,
And discovery be death.
Thus he stood there, greatly fearing
To advance or to retreat;
Wishing well the struggle over,
Be it vict'ry or defeat.
Then once more the soft voice uttered
The same language once again,
As some lovely child addressing,
In this coaxing, low refrain:
"Fannie! Fannie! come here, darling;
Come to sister, precious one!

We must hasten home to mother,
For she's lonely while we're gone."
With amazement dumb, confounded,
Heard the hunter this refrain;
Then at intervals repeated,
Came the same weird tone again,
O'er and o'er the words repeating,
With a tenderness so deep,
Was each word with pleading weighted,
They would cause a stone to weep.
And the hunter dropped his weapon.
Strong emotion shook his frame,
And his eyes were dim with weeping,
As the tears with freedom came,
Coursing down his bearded visage,
With that strong, resistless flow,
Only known when hearts are melted
By another's grief and woe.

Roused he, then, and onward started
To the troubled one's relief,
Trusting he might comfort bring her,
And assuage her heavy grief.
Softly, then, his steps advancing,
For the woods were filled with foes,
Came he near the spot, where, seeming,
To his ear, the voice arose.
Then with care the bushes parted,
And beheld a maiden fair,
Clothed with torn and tattered garments,
With unbound and streaming hair;
And with wondrous eyes, whose gleaming
Glance was fastened on a bird
Flitting round amid the branches,
From her parted lips he heard:
"Fannie! Fannie! come here, darling;
Come to sister, precious one;
We must hasten home to mother,
For she's lonely when we're gone."
But the wild bird, all unheeding,
In its joyous life so free,

The words of the little maiden,
    Flitted on from tree to tree,
And she followed, softly calling,
    O'er and o'er, her sad refrain,
And her sweet voice grew more cheerful,
    As she neared the bird again;
Till, at length, it plumed its bright wings,
    For a loftier flight away,
In the blue sky's mellow arches,
    Where alone is perfect day.
Then the ravings of the maiden,
    In her helpless, wild despair,
Filled with woeful lamentations
    All the sombre Autumn air:

"Fannie! Fannie! why, my darling
    Have you now so wilfull grown?
Why, oh darling, will you leave me
    In this dreadful place alone?
Come back, Fannie; come back, sister;
    I have found your little hood;
We must hasten home to mother,
    From this dark and dismal wood."

But no answer to her calling
    Save its echoing refrain,
Came from out the silent wildwood
    To relieve her tortured brain.
Came no soothing for her anguish,
    Came no balm for her deep grief,
Save the requiem in the branches,
    O'er the death of falling leaf.
As in sympathy the heavens
    O'er the scene drew sombre veil,
And the tender winds more sadly
    Echoed her despairing wail,
While the gloaming shadows faintly
    From the westward slowly crept,
And the ashen clouds in sorrow
    Sympathetically wept.

Then the hunter came unto her,
As she lay upon the ground,
And she knew it not; her sobbing
Shut from her all other sound.
Stood in sympathetic silence,
For no words can e'er express,
The feeling for another's woe,
For the human heart's distress.
Long he stood, 'til she grew calmer,
Until hushed became her moan,
Knowing that deep grief's a burden
All must bear and bear alone.
Then he spoke unto the maiden:
"Why girl, you're troubled," he said.

She turned her glance upon him, then,
Shrieking wildly, quickly fled
Up the steep and rugged mountain
'Til a chasm crossed her way;
Out she leaped, and at its bottom
Torn and bruised and bleeding lay.
There the hunter quickly found her,
With her heart-beats faint and low,
While from out her wounds was streaming
Fast her life in crimson flow.
From the brook he bathed her temples,
Wet her swollen, parchéd lips,
Chafed her hands, and saw the life blood
Glowing at her finger tips.
Then, to consciousness returning,
Slowly opened she her eyes,
And the glance she turned upon him
Was of wonder and surprise;
Not the weird and wildly gleaming,
When at first her voice he heard,
As she stood there in the forest,
Pleading strangely with the bird,
But a glance which spoke of reason,
Then her pain called forth a moan,
And she feebly asked the hunter:
"Why am I here and alone?"

And he said: "Rest, child, a moment,
And then tell me how you come
To be straying in this wildwood;
Where is your home? What is your name?"
Then she told him that her dear home
By a lake and river lay;
How she lost her little sister;
That her name was Mabel Gray.

Now the hunter well remembered
Lake and river, and the home,
And he wondered at the distance
The poor girl had safely come
Through the dreary, trackless forest,
Filled with savage beasts of prey.
Perchance her strongest guardian was
Her weird, wild insanity.
Then he wound his coat about her,
Lifted her with tenderness,
Started forth upon his mission,
Her lone parents' hearts to bless:
Knowing that the soul that giveth
Is the soul that liveth most;
He who others' burdens beareth
Is unto himself a host.
And the way, despite his burden,
Shortened quickly, day by day,
And grew brighter and still brighter
As he onward pushed his way,
'Til at length he climbed the mountain,
Saw the valley far below;
Saw the lake in brightness gleaming;
Heard the low-voiced river's flow.
Then he shouted with his coming,
Bounding swiftly o'er the ground:
"Rise and sing loud hallelujahs,
For behold, the lost is found!"

Found! but oh, how weak! Poor Mabel,
Helpless as a babe, new-born,
Now subsided fear and fever,
Tender limbs all bruised and torn!
There she lay upon her pillow,
Scarcely conscious of the bliss,
Which thrilled all her soul and being,
At her parents' loving kiss.
"Mabel, darling," said her mother,
"Where is Fannie?" Mabel sighed,
And unto her mother's question
For her answer thus replied:

III.

"Mother, bear with me a little —
Just a very little while;
I did cling so close to Fannie
As we clambered o'er the stile;
Then across the dusty highway,
To the grove of piñon trees,
Where the ripest nuts were falling,
Shaken by the passing breeze.
There we played, and laughed, and shouted,
In our merriment and glee —
Fannie never seemed so happy
As in playing there with me;
'Til, at length, we both grew weary,
And we laid us down to rest,
Fannie's golden head, so curly,
Pillowed safely on my breast.
And I thought me not to slumber,
But strict watch o'er sister keep,

"While she drew new strength, refreshing,
From the wonder-land of sleep.
As through interlacing branches,
Looked I on the deep blue sky,
Came a fleecy cloudlet drifting
O'er the opening slowly by.
Then the South wind breathed more warmly,
Whispered louder to the trees,
And to me 'twas sweetest music —
Half forgotten melodies!
For a moment then I listened;
Then I slowly closed mine eyes,
And the music grew far sweeter —
Like your old, sweet lullabies.
My head rested on your bosom,
Free from every care and pain,
And I felt your arms entwining
Round about my form again;
Felt your gentle fingers toying
With the ringlets on my brow;
Felt your gentle kiss, so loving,
As I do, dear mother, now.

"While, half conscious, I lay dreaming,
Felt I wave of pinions there;
Saw — or seemed to see — sweet Fannie
Wafted upward through the air.
Then I woke, and all was darkness!
All was silent! save the moan
Of the swaying trees above me —
But, oh God, I was alone!
Fannie! Fannie! called I, groping
All about the darkened wood,
But I found her not, nor nothing,
Save alone her little hood.
Called I louder; but the echo
Of my voice alone replied,

"As it bounded from the hillside,
  And then fainter grew, and died.
And the moon her face had shrouded,
  And the stars refused to shine,
On such wild and awful terror,
  As now froze this heart of mine.
And the night winds chill and clammy,
  From the marshes and the fen,
Sobbing weirdly, kissed my forehead,
  Then swept onward down the glen.
And the ivy vine, in swaying,
  Swept across my neck and face,
As a serpent to enfold me
  In its poisonous embrace.
Then the darkness grew and thickened,
  So that nothing could I see —
The heavens black and chill above,
  As the cold earth under me.
Then I held my breath to listen:
  All was silent as the dead,
Save the winds among the branches,
  Gently sighing, overhead.
Stood I long in silence, listening,
  Hoping I might hear her voice,
Calling to me from the forest,
  Bidding my sad heart rejoice.
She is, thought I, in the wildwood,
  Close behind some stump or tree;
Surely she will hear me calling,
  And come bounding forth to me.

"Fannie! Fannie! still I shouted,
  Come to sister, blessed one;
We must hasten home to mother,
  For she's lonely while we're gone.
Come to sister, little darling;
  Come, I've found your little hood;

"We must hasten home to mother,
  From this dark and dismal wood.

"Then a strange and awful trembling
    Shook me as strong winds the leaf;
  I forgot all other feeling,
    All of sorrow and of grief.
  I could see her just before me,
    Plainly as I see you now,
  With her silken, sun-kissed ringlets,
    Lying on her love-lit brow.
  Hither, thither, through the forest,
    Playing hide-and-seek with me,
  Always laughing, always cheerful,
    Full of merriment and glee.
  I saw nothing but dear Fannie,
    Until by the hunter found,
  As I lay all bruised and bleeding,
    On the cold and stony ground."

  Then, her gentle face up-turning,
    Through the window to the sky,
  Whispered: "Mother, do you think it
    Such an awful thing to die?
  Mother, I shall not be with you
    But a very little time,
  I am going to another,
    Better, sweeter, brighter clime.
  Listen! don't you hear the voices
    Speaking to us everywhere?
  Hear the leaves and flowers, in dying,
    Filling all the sky with prayer?
  Angel hosts are sweetly singing
    Melodies so soft and low;
  They are calling to me, mother,
    Calling to me now, to go.
  In their midst is little Fannie,
    Clad in robes of spotless white;

"She is smiling now a welcome—
 A pleased welcome of delight!
She is calling, 'Mabel, Mabel,
 Come to little sister now;
Come and wear a robe of beauty
 And a wreath upon your brow!'
Fannie, darling, I am coming,
 Coming to you, blessed one!
And we'll watch and wait for mother,
 'Til the angels bid her come.
Sweeter, sweeter grows the music,
 Brighter, brighter grows the sky;
Hear the waving of their pinions—
 Good-bye, mother; all, good-bye!"

* * *

And they laid her in the valley,
 Underneath the woodland trees,
Where at morning and at evening,
 Sinks to rest the woodland breeze.
Clouds of Winter o'er the brown earth
 A soft mantle wove of snow,
Still of little Fannie's dark fate
 They no certainty could know,
Until low-voiced Spring came bringing
 Her sweet birds and blooming flowers,
And earth's garments green were woven
 By the sunshine and the showers.
Save the pine tree by the blue lake,
 Where the eagles built their nest,
All the countless trees around it,
 Were in garments richly dressed.

But, like a blackened skeleton,
    From which all power of life had fled,
It stood among its fellow trees
    Alone, loveless, leafless, dead.
And, at length, beneath the woodman's
    Keen-edged axe, it quickly fell,
And the secret, so well hidden,
    Did thus by its falling tell:
In the eagle's nest was woven,
    With the moss and grasses there —
Startling him who did behold them —
    Silken strands of golden hair.

BLOSSOMS AND BRIERS

CALIFORNIA

THOSE EYES OF BROWN

THOSE EYES OF BROWN.

In all the world there is but one
Pair of eyes of brown,
That are more beauteous than the sun
When it goes down.
They shine at morn, at noon, at night,
Always for me,
With love's enchanting, trustful light
Of harmony.

Beside those eyes the star-beams shine
But languid, dull;
To me their light is all divine —
Most wonderful!
And when their curtains softly fall,
So coyly down,
I love them more than life, than all —
Those eyes of brown.

When crimson blushes upward sweep
O'er lips and face,
And slowly from her fair cheeks creep
With matchless grace,
Were I possessed of all the earth —
A royal crown!
I'd give it all to match their worth —
Those eyes of brown.

In them sweet Summer ever shines,
And fair flowers bloom;
There Pleasure stores her richest mines—
In them is room
For every thought of peace and love
My life to crown,
With joys surpassing heaven's above —
Those eyes of brown.

WAITING.

I sit alone within my room,
  While evening shadows softly fall,
Filling each nook about with gloom,
  And slowly creep athwart the wall;
The clock in doleful silence ticks
        The hour of six.

The ruddy fire all brightly burns;
  The stand near by with open books;
An empty easy-chair which yearns
  For some one's coming — so it looks;
I count each moment as 'tis given,
        'Til hour of seven.

I pace the floor with measured tread,
  And ear attentive to each sound;
A doubt creeps in — a thought of dread —
  Her footsteps are not homeward bound;
How can it be she stays so late?
        The clock strikes eight!

Footsteps! Ah, surely she is come!
  I haste to greet her at the door,
But all without again is dumb,
  Though I call to her o'er and o'er,
I cannot glean of her a sign;
        The clock strikes nine!

Oh, anxious heart, be still, be calm;
  Though cloud-tears mark the window pane,
Thy waiting sweetens but the balm
  That she will bring thee through the rain.
That she will bring me? Ah, but when?
        The clock strikes ten!

WAITING.

Now drag the night-hours slowly by;
  The fire within the grate low burns;
My fevered lips are parched and dry,
  My wretched heart, oh, how it yearns!
A hell, where might have been a heaven!
        The clock strikes 'leven!

My eyes close slowly, and my head
  Will droop upon my weary breast;
Some Siren with the rain is wed —
  She sings so sweetly now of rest.
Into life's mystery I delve —
        The clock strikes twelve.

How peaceful and how light my heart!
  How beautiful all things now seem!
Swiftly the evening hours depart,
  And firesides warmly, brightly gleam;
All cares are banished with the sun.
        The clock strikes one.

I hear a footstep at the door!
  Into my arms in haste she springs,
And love expresses o'er and o'er,
  As to my breast she sweetly clings.
Sweetheart! How loving and how true!
        The clock strikes two.

We chat beside the glowing fire,
  And read some stanzas from the book;
Love leaves unanswered no desire,
  But speaks in every tone and look;
Life seems one dazzling, love-lit sea —
        The clock strikes three.

She sings so sweetly the old songs;
  I kiss her shining hair and eyes;
She coyly says: "To thee belongs
  These lips." I answer with replies,
Perhaps a dozen, if not more.
        The clock strikes four.

We kneel again at evening prayer,
  Silent, beside our snowy bed:
Oh, God, our every secret share,
  And our fond hearts more firmly wed;
Bring us to thee; for this we strive —
    The clock strikes five.

The gray dawn streams across the sky;
  How cold! how cold! Mamie, my dear,
Art waking, love? but no reply:
  My God! a dream! she is not here.
Laugh, fiends! and hemlock-juices mix —
    The clock strikes six.

THE RULE TO LIVE.

"As Thou wilt, Lord," young Robin said,
  And each day said anew,
And walked in paths of pleasantness,
  To manhood firm and true.

Each morn to him was God's rich gift —
  An opportunity,
To aid his fellow mortals on,
  O'er life's tempestuous sea.

He loved not riches to exclude,
  From out his honest mind,
The fairest flowers and richest fruits,
  Bestowed upon mankind.

But in their season of them all,
  To uses good applied,
And all who knew him, loved him well,
  And mourned him when he died.

Be kind, be generous, be true,
  And unto others give,
A life which daily proves itself
  A blessing while you live.

MY WORLD.

I have a world—'tis all my own,
  More beautiful and fair to see,
Than aught this world has ever known—
  Where all is love and purity.

Its rivers broad, its purling rills,
  With music sweet the soul delight;
Its lovely, mist-enshrouded hills,
  Are ever charming to my sight.

Its mountains rear majestically,
  Far, far aloft, their regal heads,
Where sport soft Summer winds at play,
  And soul with angel-spirit weds.

Its broad, high plains of active thought,
  Where every breath expands the soul;
Where every pleasure comes unsought,
  And youth remains while ages roll.

Where ever glows the sun of peace,
  Where blooms affection's fairest flowers;
Where love and hope and trust increase,
  With endless flight of Summer hours.

A cottage on the hillside stands,
  O'erlooking meadows decked with flowers,
And spirit forms with magic wands,
  Enchant and bless the golden hours.

About the door the ivy clings,
  And with its slender tendrils weave
A magic pattern, which it flings
  At either side, along the eaves.

About its windows blooms the rose,
  Which fills the air with sweet perfume,
And woos the sense to sweet repose,
  When falls the evening's quiet gloom.

A mother sits within the door,
  With mother love her face most fair;
While sunlight glinting o'er the floor,
  Falls on a cherub sleeping there.

A brown-eyed boy with golden hair,
  With chubby hands and dimpled chin,
And soul as pure as Heaven's air,
  Where falleth no dark shade of sin.

How my poor heart doth for them yearn,
  To fold them to my bosom now;
And kiss them each again, in turn,
  On ruby lips and love-lit brow!

I love the night, for then it seems
  They come with love's sweet smile to me,
And in those dear, enchanted dreams,
  I live in true reality.

EDENS I'M SEEKING TO FIND.

Come, sit here, my friend, while I draw back the curtain,
  Which hangs o'er my heart and its secrets enfold
Of mysteries deep, and strange feelings uncertain,
  Which slowly, but surely, are making me old.

I would I were able in language to utter,
  And speak forth my thought, that you might understand,
But the best I can do is only to mutter —
  For language is dull, save the glance and the hand.

From youth all my soul has been rocked with emotions,
  Which roll like a troubled sea over my mind ;
And strange winds have whispered, from over deep oceans,
  Which tell me of Edens I'm longing to find.

On the wings of these winds, a sweet, tender spirit
  Has spoken, at times, a sweet peace to my soul ;
I longingly listen, all prayerful, to hear it —
  'Tis drowned in the busy world's bustle and roll !

MY MOTHER.

I speak of one who, 'neath the sun,
Embodies every grace,
And every virtue plainly is
Depicted in her face;
To whom the gods have given form,
Above all human kind ;
A jewel rare, beyond compare —
The setting of her mind.

Her loving smile all cares beguile,
And fills me with delight ;
With her my days are pleasure's own,
And peaceful every night;
To whom the gods a charm hath given,
Bequeathed unto no other ;
There is not — ne'er can be again,
An equal to my mother.

FOR THOSE WE LOVE.

How sweet to feel we're going home:
To calmly look to the beyond,
From whence our sweetest visions come,
And lasting treasures may be found.

Where holy triumphs rest secure,
And joys and pleasures never die;
Where dwelleth naught that is impure,
In love's sweet home, beyond the sky.

'Tis not for self--oh no, not so,
But for the souls of those we love;
For them, dear Lord, oh, let us grow
Immortal in the fields above.

Bestow on us immortal life,
And wipe away all bitter tears;
Shut out all fear and thought of strife,
Let shine the flood of golden years.

My Heart is Strangely Sad To-night.

My heart is strangely sad to-night,
I would not hear thee sing;
The songs which once were my delight,
With discords harshly ring.

I love the songs of other days,
Heard at my mother's knee;
Would walk again youth's pleasant ways —
Alone, in memory.

Oh, mother! come again to me,
And soothe my weary heart;
I still am but a child to thee,
Whate'er to others art.

My soul cries out in weariness,
To pillow on thy breast—
To calm this pain and deep distress,
And with thee sweetly rest.

Weep on, tired heart, thy sad refrain,
So tremulous and low,
Swept by the cruel hand of pain,
No mortal ear may know.

Thy grief, thy woe, thy bitter tears,
No mortal eye may see,
But He will bless in coming years,
Who rules eternity.

Life.

Life is a wave on which men rise,
To seize ambition's tinsel crown;
All other pleasures loathe, despise,
To win one smile from fleeting fame,
Then sink beneath death's waters down
And cease to live, save in a name.

BIRD SONG.

Sweetheart, sweetheart, sweetheart, sweet, sweet, sweet,
Caroled forth a wild bird, gaily,
As it flitted here and there,
Through the blithesome Spring-time daily,
Where the trees their blossoms wear;
Morning, evening, all the day,
It seemed ever thus to say:
Sweetheart, sweetheart, sweetheart, sweet, sweet, sweet.

Sweetheart, sweetheart, sweetheart, sweet, sweet, sweet,
Filling all the air about me,
With its joyous notes of song,
'Til each motion of the air-sea
Seemed to roll with joy along.
Light my heart and bright the day,
When I heard the sweet bird say:
Sweetheart, sweetheart, sweetheart, sweet, sweet, sweet.

Sweetheart, sweetheart, sweetheart, sweet, sweet, sweet,
The words kept ringing in my ears,
And they filled my heart with joy,
'Til moistened were my eyes with tears,
But no grief did them alloy,
For I wended swift my way,
To my love, that I might say:
Sweetheart, sweetheart, sweetheart, sweet, sweet, sweet.

FAITHFUL TO THE END.

You've come again, old friend, to me,
To keep the vows of other years;
I've kept thy love safe in my heart,
Embalmed in sorrows and in tears.
True love can never, never change,
Though sorrows, troubles be its fate,
Now, after all these weary years,
To think your coming is too late.

Come, dear, and fold me to your breast,
  And take this feeble hand in thine,
And let me hear the sweet old voice,
  Say that you truly now art mine.
Our paths through life have lain apart,
  And now life's sun is sinking low;
Come, press me, darling, to your heart,
  And kiss me once before I go.

There, darling, do not weep for me;
  The weary hours have almost flown;
And this sweet meeting now with thee,
  Heals all the sorrows I have known.
Still tread the path of life alone,
  We've just a few more years to wait;
I'll watch, and long, and pray for thee,
  And keep ajar the golden gate.

I've watched and waited, wept and prayed,
  That you would quickly, quickly come,
Through all these lonely, weary years;
  But now I pray: "God's will be done."
I dreamed that we would happy be,
  And was content to watch and wait;
But dreams alone, alas! they'll be,
  For now your coming is too late.

Farewell, for I must leave you now;
  I hear the angels' welcome call;
Come closer, for my sight grows dim,
  The dews of death upon me fall.
Good-bye, old love, a last good-bye,
  I'm going from this world of pain;
I'll watch, and wait, and pray for thee,
  Till we in heaven meet again.

COME WITH THY HARP

Come with thy harp at evening's hour,
    When hungry grows the heart for love,
And let me feel its melting pow'r,
    My soul to soothe.

When care and strife die on the air,
 And passing moments breathe of peace,
Oh, let me feel thy presence there,
 That doubts may cease.

Let thy hand softly touch the strings,
 That waken fondest dreams of mine,
And by low pleading always brings
 My soul to thine.

The evening zephyr's softest tone,
 Faintly perfumed by breath of flowers,
Is fitting messenger, my own,
 For love like ours.

MY FRIEND.

Words compass not a richer thought
 Than this: He is my friend;
One who stands firm and true, unbought,
 Steadfast unto the end;
Who speaks a word of kindness, when
 The world in anger frowns;
For him my heart in fealty then,
 With all its being crowns.

No gift to mortal man is given,
 So sweet, so rich as this;
It rivals e'en the hope of Heaven,
 With all its wondrous bliss,
To fully trust, to feel and know,
 Unto the bitter end,
Whate'er may happen here below,
 He is my steadfast friend.

To feel and know his strong right arm
 Is bared in my defense,
To shield and guard from every harm,
 Whate'er the consequence,
Fills full my cup, unto the brim,
 With joys that sweetly blend,
And makes myself, second to him,
 Who truly is my friend.

MY MOTHER'S DEATH.

"So tired, let me rest," mother sighed, as she wearily
Moaned in her weakness and closed her dear eyes,
That had for a moment looked outward so drearily,
Over the meadows, and up to the skies:
The soft, azure skies, where fleecy clouds drifted,
As idly, dreamily onward they rolled,
While bright, mellow sunbeams lazily sifted
Through them, to the earth, a shimmer of gold.
Then Silence laid heavily on us his finger,
And grief filled our bosoms at thought of the pall,
And the death angel's visit, who let her still linger,
A short measure with us, ere making his call.

He delayed but a moment: so soft was his coming,
We thought that dear mother but quietly slept,
While nothing we heard, save the honey-bees' humming,
As through the open window their low voices crept.
Then o'er her wan features death's presence came creeping;
We pressed down her eyelids, and folded her hands;
Then low words were spoken to comfort the weeping,
And tell of her welcome in heavenly lands.
We robed her loved form with the sepulcher's dressing,
And lowered her so lovingly down by the side,
Of him whom her heart, while he lived, was confessing
The love of her life, which bloomed on till she died.

They rest on a wave, which arose from the ocean,
And beat back the waters to river and sea:
An emerald wave of the prairie, whose motion,
Has slumbered since, fanned by the glad winds so free.
The last golden rays of the day-beams, when dying,
Kissed gently their graves with soft light as they fell,
And again to the world we turned with deep sighing,
As sadly we bade them a loving farewell.
There in peace let them rest, heart to heart, dust to dust,
Until the Lord's coming in glory again:
For He was their shepherd, their hope, and their trust—
The Saviour, to them, of the children of men.

THE STATUE TO PYGMALEON.

Gaze on, oh soul of love, gaze on,
  Speak with thy fervent glance, and give
This marble form, this heart of stone,
  The strength and power to move and live.

Beneath that gaze I live, I see,
  Thou my creator and my friend;
Love boundless as eternity,
  Thy every glance and movement blend.

By love's divine, empowering glow,
  This marble form with life is thrilled;
I feel the rich blood's quickening flow,
  With throbbing life my bosom filled.

Love is of life the only worth,
  It is my heart, my soul, my breath,
The quickening power which gave me birth;
  Be it withdrawn, I sleep in death.

THE EVENING OF LIFE.

The snows of the Winter of life, old man,
    Have fallen upon your hair,
And the breath of Summer's soft, wooing winds,
    Comes not to disturb them there.
Your step has grown feeble, and bowed your form;
    Now trembles your palsied hand;
But a few short years since you stood erect,
    The stalwart of all the land!

But the hours of the gloaming of life, old man,
    For you have come gently on;
Is the evening of life to you, old man,
    As sweet as its early dawn?
Is the golden light of life's setting sun
    As bright as its morning ray?
Are the hours of closing as dear, old man,
    As those in the heat of day?

Has the western slope of the hill, old man,
For you a September sky?
Has life's setting sun a soft, mellow light,
As the night of death draws nigh?
Does your path grow smooth, as it nears the shore,
The shore of the mystic sea?
Do its billowy waves an anthem sing —
The waves of eternity?

For your soul, thank God, your great soul, old man,
Beams forth from your clear, blue eye,
With a power which tells of the light in man
That never was born to die,
And your face is lit with a beaming smile,
Well knowing your work is done;
That the pains, and sorrows, and trials of life
Shall cease with its setting sun?

Does your star of hope now more brightly shine,
Dispelling the gloom of the grave?
Are the waters of death now clear to you,
Silver crested every wave?
Rejoice! your journey is over, old man,
Pass to the shores of the blest;
Thou hast fought the battle of life, old man,
Enter thou into thy rest.

CUPID'S BLOSSOMS.

I've seen thee oft when roses wreathed
About thy features, garlands bright;
When thy fair bosom fondly breathed
In ecstasy of pure delight.

When thy brown eyes with pleasure shone —
Your lips were red with passion's glow,
And knew thy heart was all my own,
When love was one unbroken flow.

WHEN I AM OLD.

When shadows came not to annoy
Our perfect harmony of bliss;
When every pulse was one of joy,
Making our life all loveliness.

Since then I've seen the roses fade,
And in their place pale lilies lay;
Oh, shame! to think fair, lovely maid,
That I had chased their bloom away.

Oh, dearest maid, I do confess,
I have those roses falsely slain;
But, darling, come and let me kiss
Those blooms of Cupid back again!

WHEN I AM OLD.

Oh, love and song, I pray thee stay
And bless my later years;
Pass not, I pray, with youth away,
And leave but sorrow's tears;
Let not my heart grow chill and cold,
When I am old.

When I am old I'll need thee more,
For when the shadows call,
And I have numbered my three score,
And leaves of Autumn fall —
Do thou my heart and life enfold.
When I am old.

When I am old, how soon 'twill be!
The years fly swiftly past,
And drop into eternity —
This one may be my last!
May pleasures e'er their sweets unfold
To all the old.

LITTLE CUPID.

Toy with his golden hair;
    Kiss him again,
On his pure brow so fair,
On his sweet eyelids there,
    Shower them like rain.

Let his sweet laughter ring,
    Let his bright eyes
Their piercing arrows fling,
And to our hearts still bring
    Soft Summer skies.

OH LET ME DREAM.

Welcome, welcome, beautiful night!
With mantle of gloom and golden stars,
And gentle moon, whose mellow light,
Glistens and gleams in silver bars.
Now let me sleep; oh, let me dream,
Under the stars —
Bright, lovely stars,
Venus and Mars,
Sweet, beaming stars,
As they now shine, and sparkling gleam,
Oh, let me dream
Of love — sweet love,
Love from above,
Oh, let me dream
Of love.

Oh, Morpheus! thine arms entwine,
And fold me lightly to thy breast,
And let me dream of love divine,
Through all my hours of quiet rest.
Oh, let me sleep; oh, let me dream,
Under the stars —
Bright, lovely stars,
Venus and Mars,
Sweet, beaming stars,
As they now shine, and sparkling gleam,
Oh, let me dream
Of love — sweet love,
Love from above,
Oh, let me dream
Of love.

DUALITY.

The bush which boasts the fairest rose,
Likewise doth yield the sharpest thorn;
The lips which honeyed sweetness knows,
Are often curled in bitter scorn.

LOVE'S LONGING.

Oh, loved one, do you know how I long
    To meet you, and clasp you, my own,
And feel the sweet thrill of joy,
    To none but the true lover known?
To fold you again to my breast,
    To kiss those dear lips as of yore,
And hear them lisp the sweet words:
  "I am thine, only thine, evermore!"

Oh, darling, 'tis so hard to wait —
    To wait without knowing how long
'Twill be, ere the morning light breaks,
    And life be one sweet, endless song;
A round of the dearest of joys,
    Each moment be laden with bliss,
Each hour be to trouble unknown,
    Each day open and close with a kiss.

When clouds, which hang over our sky,
    Shall roll far away to the West,
And we, in the full joy of love,
    Shall richly and sweetly be blessed;
When this dull, endless aching shall cease,
    And our hearts throb with great beats of joy,
And our lives shall in every part,
    Know naught of regret or alloy.

Oh, love, 'twould be heaven below,
    To ever have you at my side;
To call you and kiss you, my own,
    My angel, my darling, my bride.
Oh, haste thee, oh, haste, Father Time,
    Thy chariot wheels move so slow;
Oh, haste thee, and bring us the hour,
    When this joy we fully may know.

PLUCK THE ROSES ERE THEY DIE.

Pluck the roses, lovely roses,
  While they're blooming fresh and fair;
While their sweet life still discloses
  A wealth of fragrance on the air.

Take the gifts which God has given,
  Each one in season as they come;
They will make this earth a heaven,
  A peaceful, sweet and happy home.

All the world is filled with beauty,
  By God prepared to charm the eye;
'Tis of life a pleasant duty —
  Pass not a thing of beauty by.

Drink at every crystal fountain —
  The wine of life flows freely now;
Let each breeze from sea and mountain
  With kisses cool thy fevered brow.

WHO CAME TO ME IN MY DREAM.

Who came to me in my dream?
It was she; it was she,
Who alone holds the key.
Of my heart's door for me —
She came to me in my dream.

Who came to me in my dream?
'Twas a heavenly visitant,
By the angels' sweet consent,
One of their own element —
She came to me in my dream.

Who came to me in my dream?
She, the one of all the earth —
She, the one of beauty's birth,
She, the one of matchless worth —
She came to me in my dream.

LOVE'S GOLDEN HOURS.

Come, let us watch the golden day,
You, dearest love, and I;
Behold the last smile fade away
Upon the azure sky.

And listen to the evening wind,
Sighing so soft and low,
For the sweet moments left behind —
That they so swiftly go.

Come, let us cull from those that pass,
The sweets they have in store,
For when they're gone, no power, alas!
Their blessings can restore.

These are the golden hours of love,
When heart speaks unto heart;
When lustrous stars from heaven above,
Their trembling glance impart,

To light the world with ray serene,
When all is kind and still,
And o'er the sweet and peaceful scene,
Throw powers that chain the will.

MY LOVE.

Beloved! when sorrows shroud my troubled soul,
And life seems one great gulf of deep despair;
When clouds of storm upon me fiercely roll,
And livid lightenings rend the humid air,
And I can hear the nearer breakers roar,
As eager to devour their helpless prey,
I, fainting, drop the helm and oar,
As glimmering fades hope's sympathizing ray.
A radiant vision then dispels the gloom,
And through the clouds angelic loveliness —
Thy form — more fair than Hope's most radiant bloom,
Appears, my drooping soul to cheer and bless.

FIRST HOURS OF LOVE.

Oh, let me live them o'er again!
    The hours when first I loved;
When first enchanting through my brain,
Enraptured passion's lovely train,
    Bewilderingly moved!

Oh, rapturous joy! oh, love divine!
    In virgin purity,
Again through all my being shine,
My soul in her's again entwine,
    In sweet security!

Oh, could I feel as then I felt,
    My life, my soul I'd give,
To have all troubling dross to melt,
Before sweet love as then it dwelt,
    Ah, then 'twas sweet to live!

Alas! to me they'll never come;
    They are forever fled;
Search where I will, where'er I roam,
Their flitting shadows in the gloam,
    Remind me they are dead!

Ghosts of a joy, of moments dead,
    Which never from me rove;
Though they be now forever fled,
By mem'ry still my soul is wed
    To thoughts of early love.

WHY CHIDE ME?

Ye chide me that I love no more
And answer not your sigh with sighs,
And feel no more your loving power?
Remember, love, the sweetest flower
Once blooms, then dies.

I LOVE THEE STILL.

Oh, darling! could I voice my sorrow,
Or speak the thoughts my bosom fill;
Thou sure would'st know, ere gleams the morrow,
That with my soul — I love thee still.

Since first thy kindly glance beholding,
Love's stream has flown, a sparkling rill;
My every thought thy life enfolding,
Oh, locks of jet! — I love thee still.

Why should love's sea, with gentle heaving,
Now with rough waves thy bosom fill?
Oh, love! I faint, I die with grieving;
God knows my heart — I love thee still.

Oh, look not, love, with cold disdaining
Upon me; for I have no will,
Save that of my lost heaven regaining,
When thou shalt say: — "I love thee still!"

AS FIRST I SAW THEE.

As first I saw thee, darling one,
I see thee still to-night!
Of all that group 'tis thee alone,
That dwells still in my sight.
All else has faded from my skies,
By memory forgot:
Passed from the vision of my eyes,
And is as though 'twere not.

It may be that thy loving smile,
And glance of thy bright eye,
Hast so engrossed my thoughts, erstwhile,
All else did'st fade and die.
Howe'er it be, this much, I know,
Undoubtedly is true:
Where'er I be, where'er I go,
I see — I love but you.

OH SLUMBER, MY DARLING.

Oh slumber, my darling ! oh, slumber away
The sweet hours of rest, until soft morning gray
Shall with sun-kisses wake thee,
From sweet dreams of thy love
To the blessed reality,
Which shall far sweeter prove.

Oh, talk not of dreams to those who have loved,
A far sweeter passion hath their hearts moved !
Sweeter joys, brighter gleams
O'er their pathway doth fall,
Than lies in the power of dreams,
E'en of love, to recall.

IMMORTAL LOVE.

There is an end to flowers and birds,
To grazing flocks and lowing herds;
An end to all things 'neath the skies,
To rosy lips and sparkling eyes;
And end to laughter and to mirth,
To all, save one sweet thing on earth,
There is an end.

There is an end to night and day,
All things of earth shall pass away,
But there is one thing 'neath the sky,
That, surely, was not born to die.
No change can harm its fervent breath;
It liveth on till after death—
It can not die.

It lives beyond the silent grave,
Where orange fair and palm trees wave—
'Tis sung by heaven's angelic choir—
The echoing notes of sacred lyre
Come floating down in dreams to me,
And whisper: "Through eternity,
It shall ever be."

RUTH.

Dear form — sweet face — bright hair,
    My love for thee is one
Sweet, fervent breath of prayer,
    Ne'er ending since begun.

Begun as soon as sight,
    From those dear eyes to mine,
Shot glances of delight,
    Wedding my soul to thine.

By laws as fixed at birth,
    As pleasure or of pain,
Or any of the earth —
    Thy soul doth mine contain.

As flowers to the sun,
    As rivers to the sea,
As Time flows ever on,
    My soul doth turn to thee.

My sorrows, tears and grief
    Vanish before thy face,
And perfect, sweet relief
    Sits smiling in their place.

When thou art gone, the sun
    Shines dimly on my path,
And all the fleecy clouds
    Seem turned to frowns of wrath.

The birds sing not so sweet,
    And weary is their song;
Their notes do harshly greet
    Mine ears, and seem too long.

'Tis strange, but yesterday,
    When thou wert here, their notes
Seemed streams of melody,
    Pouring from silver throats.

The sunlight's golden gleam,
    The fleecy cloudlets' sail,
Were shimmering, pulsing stream,
    And lovely bridal veil.

Morn, noon and night I raise
    My soul to God in prayer,
And thankfulness and praise,
    And plead his tender care,

To guard thy precious head
    From every source of harm,
And o'er thy slumbering bed
    To stretch His mighty arm.

Love lives beyond the tomb;
    In heaven, pure and free,
Its sweet flowers ever bloom,
    In immortality.

THE LOVER'S LAMENT.

How sad my heart, for thou art gone,
    While evening shadows round me fall,
And find me silent and alone,
    As I the loving past recall.

How yearns my heart to call thee back,
    To nestle in these arms again!
Oh, haste, retrace the foamy track —
    Recross the dark and raging main!

The sky is set with glinting stars,
    But not one ray is shed for me;
My sorrow all their light debars,
    My star of hope sank in the sea.

The raging billows clasped her where
    No mortal hand could close her eyes;
Her helpless cry of wild despair
    Was echoed by the sea-birds' cries.

The wild waves clasped her to their breast,
    And wound about her form so fair,
And gently down her eyelids pressed;
    Toyed as a lover with her hair.

And kissed her lips, as lovers kiss —
    Ah, madly! till her fragrant breath
Was given up in answering bliss,
    And her sweet form lay cold in death.

IN MEMORY OF HON. JOHN B. FINCH.

Lo! he is dead;
This brilliant leader of our cause;
This brave defender of the right;
This advocate of purer laws,
Who charmed and filled us with delight;
Can he be dead?

Ah, who could know
That he we loved and cherished so
Would, in the brightest hour of life,
With intellect and soul aglow,
Amid the conflict and the strife
Be stricken low?

We stand aghast,
To think his life is o'er and past,
While yet his sun was at its noon;
It's brightest rays should be its last,
And midnight's chill and silent gloom
O'er him be cast.

Illustrious dead,
Sleep well; of thee 'twill e'er be said,
"He did what mortal man could do
Mankind with truth to firmly wed,
Their souls with honor to imbue,
In error's stead."

WHAT THE BIRD SAID.

A wild bird said unto its mate:
Sweetheart so pretty, sweet, sweet, sweet.
I'll sing for thee early and late,
Repeating ever sweet, sweet, sweet.

UNFORGIVEN.

At morning, at evening, at midnight,
Each hour of the days passing by,
I longingly wait for your coming,
But nothing I hear save the sigh
Which comes from the depths of my bosom --
Of hope and of joy, a deep moan,
Which tells of their absence forever —
Thy spirit hath flown!

I call to you, love, in my sorrow,
And plead with the strength of my soul,
That you will forgive me, my darling,
And stay these great billows, that roll;
That blind me, and crush me, my darling,
And leave me all wretched and prone;
Like fire flames of Hell about me,
They mock at my moan.

Your likeness I see e'er before me:
Those full cherry lips and brown eyes,
They ever have smiled me a welcome;
This Heaven, dark fate, now denies.
I see in their look "Unforgiven,"
Which wrings from my soul a deep groan;
Thus shut from the light of my Heaven,
I'm dying alone.

Oh, darling! come quick, or I perish!
Come, quick, and relieve this poor heart;
But speak to me, darling, and save me;
Oh, bid this great sorrow depart!
God knows I had loved you unceasing,
Since first thy loved face I have known;
Have worshiped and prayed, oh, believe me,
For thee, love, alone.

A RARE FLOWER.

Love is a blossom seldom seen,
No orchid half so pure and rare;
While Passion's flowers bestrew the green
And cast their odors everywhere.

DEATH SHADOWS.

Come closer, darling; hold fast my hand,
For night comes on, though the morning sun
His triumphal march has just begun,
And with dazzling light fills all the land.
Death kisses my brow;
Let your sweet presence comfort me now.

Lay close to mine your beautiful cheek;
Kiss me tenderly; let your dear eyes
Tell of the love that within them lies;
Let soul to soul in confidence speak;
For I hear the roar
Of Death's dark waters laving the shore.

Smooth down my pillow with gentle touch;
Pray I may be as a little child,
As trusting and pure and undefiled;
For the Father hath spoken of such
His chosen shall be
With Him to dwell through eternity.

MEMORY IS MINE.

Love, sweet Love, oh let me woo thee,
Though it may be all in vain;
Still, oh still let me pursue thee,
Though we may not speak again.

Give me one last smile to brighten
My lone path through future years;
Give it, Love, my load to lighten,
And to dry my bitter tears.

Go, and may God bless thee ever
With His richest gifts divine;
Though we bid farewell forever,
Still sweet Memory is mine!

By it, on my heart, your loving
Face is painted clear and bright;
Every line, so true, thus proving
How precious thou art in my sight.

TO A LOVELY MAID.

Warm rosy lips, with love-kisses laden,
  Sweeter than nectar distilled from the rose,
Dearer to me than all of life's splendors,
  The world to my heart, beside, can disclose.

Blue eyes so bright, with love glances tender,
  Piercing my bosom and thrilling my soul;
Causing pure waves of heavenly pleasure,
  Over my being in sweetness to roll.

Give me thy love, oh, sweet maid of beauty:
  I care not, on earth, what then may betide;
'Tis now my highest and only ambition,
  To kiss you and call you my own darling bride.

LOVELY FAIRY ISABEL.

Lovely fairy Isabel,
What thou art I cannot tell.
Seemingly thou art divine,
For all graces in thee shine;
For a moment with thy smile,
All my cares thou dost beguile.
Can I trust thee, Isabel?
Can I trust thee; who can tell?

Meanest what that dreamy look?
All my soul its glances shook;
Meanest what that smile of thine?
Pray oblige me and define,
For in thy bewitching eyes,
Riddles lie I cannot read;
Love is dull, and blind, unwise,
Will not give to wisdom heed;
Yet I'll trust thee, Isabel,
I will trust thee; doubt, farewell!

THE LOVER'S DESPAIR.

Oh, locks of jet! oh, soulful eyes!
Oh, lips of love! oh, form divine!
My hope, my all, my paradise!
Thy presence thrills me like rich wine.

Why has the Winter of Despair
Fallen upon our Summer scene?
Why livid lightnings rend the air
And wither all that's fresh and green?

Each flower lies broken in its bloom;
Each joy seems blasted at its morn:
Each path around leads to the tomb;
Each sound a curse that I was born.

And pallid grief forever weeps
Her scalding tears, with sob and sigh,
And Terror, like a dragon, creeps
With hideous form before my eye!

Ah, there the horrid vision comes!
Gods! take the damnéd curse away!
It chills my soul! my heart benumbs,
And turns to hell Life's golden day!

Oh! I was once so free from care,
My life a pure, unsullied page,
And sweetest joys bloomed everywhere,
Ere Sorrow's pangs had brought me age.

GEMS.

Language is but the clasp that holds
The gems of thought alone;
The plainest setting e'er unfolds
The best light of the stone.

MY BRIDE.

Eyes in whose light love's gentle glow
  Shines with a fondness, soft and pure,
Expressing all the heart may know,
  When knowing all it may endure.
Such eyes are her's: clear windows they,
  Through which her soul speaks all divine;
No lurking shadows they betray,
  But speak out frankly unto mine.

Lips rich as rosebuds in first bloom,
  Half parted in expectancy;
For loving kisses—waiting room
  For words of greeting, unto me.
Such lips are hers: the ruby wine,
  Which blushing in the grape we see,
Till plucked from the ambrosial vine,
  So waits her sweetness all for me.

A form beyond the skill to mould,
  Of all the sculptors in the land;
Her hair a softened sheen of gold,
  A study for the gods her hand.
Her joyous laughter music makes,
  Like mountain brooks, when in their glee,
Their foaming waters, sweetly wakes
  To cadence of pure minstrelsy.

CAROLINE.

My love is all for thee,
    Caroline;
Thou art all things to me—
A calm and placid sea,
Where soft winds lovingly
Breathe sweetest melody,
    All divine.

A rich gift from heavenly powers,
    Caroline;
A fresh breath of blooming flowers,
And sweet, pleasant Summer hours,
Which my thirsty soul devours
    Like rich wine.

MARY DEAN'S FIRST KISS.

We sat upon the sofa, Mary Dean
And I, who was her lover, she my queen;
I looked upon her fondly, and her eyes
Sent back to mine a wealth of love replies;
No words were spoken as I stroked her fair,
Soft, wavy hair.

The touch did thrill unto my very soul,
As waves of sweet affection o'er me stole;
Her brow, her eyes, her soft, rose-tinted lips,
All other forms of beauty did eclipse,
Crowning her wealth of beauty rare—
Her auburn hair.

Eternity may hold sweet things in store,
But to my life there cometh never more
A joy so perfect in its bliss as this
Which thrilled my soul at Mary Dean's first kiss;
As in the gloaming hours in silence there,
I stroked her hair.

HELÉNE.

I will cull for thee a bouquet, Heléne,
    To lay on thy wanton breast;
It fitted shall be, with its crimson stain,
    To deck such a viper's nest.

I will pluck it with utmost care, Heléne,
    Each part shall be all complete,
And it shall a likeness to thee contain —
    Full rounded as thy deceit.

Some sprigs of thistle and thorn, Heléne,
    A twig of the poison oak,
Entwined with the ivy — a brilliant vein,
    All fit for thy hands to stroke.

All fitted for thee to caress, Heléne,
    To receive thy slimy kiss,
Though a viler poison to heart and brain,
    Will breed from thy loathsomeness.

Polluting and foul to the touch, Heléne,
    More bitter than words can tell;
Its odors all reeking with pungent pain
    And vile as the fumes of hell.

The asp and the adder shall find, Heléne,
    A cover in every leaf;
The breath of the upas tree's deadly bane
    Shall quicken each fang for grief.

Regret and Remorse, like bloodhounds, Heléne,
    Shall follow thy guilty soul;
The scent shall grow warmer, though tears like rain
    Should over thy footprints roll.

When thy soul in terror shall flee, Heléne,
    From the body it doth degrade,
Though pregnant with curses of deepest pain,
    'Twill fall to a blacker shade.

The breath of Regret and Remorse, Heléne,
Will Memory fan to flame,
Till thy shameless soul be driven insane
At sound of thy guilty name!

To-morrow's page is unwritten, Heléne,
Unmarked by the steps of Time;
It may a record of honor retain
Unsoiled by an act of crime.

Thy delicate hands to-morrow, Heléne,
May feel not the prick of thorn;
Thy life may begin its hope to regain
With flush of the early morn.

Thou yet, perchance, may be peaceful, Heléne,
And better than thou hast been;
A name may be thine thou wilt not disdain —
The name of a Magdalen.

JANE.

Jennie, Jennie, handsome Jennie,
Eyes of brown, and auburn hair;
Blithe and merry, winsome Jennie,
With no cloud of doubt or care,
Always happy,
Oh, so happy!
Knowing naught of grief or pain;
Thou art pretty,
Gay and witty,
Youthful, singing, laughing Jane.

Jennie, Jennie, dancing Jennie,
Bright as flowers in Summer time —
Nimble as a spendthrift's penny,
Fair as blooms of any clime.
Trusting ever,
Doubting never,
Pure in heart and clear in brain,
None above thee,
How I love thee!
My own precious, darling Jane.

Jennie, Jennie, darling Jennie,
With thy wealth of shining curls;
Queen thou art, oh, fairest Jennie,
Of the world's bright throng of girls.
First in beauty,
First in duty,
Nature left thee naught to gain.
Undeceiving,
All believing,
Trusting, truthful, honest Jane.

Jennie, Jennie, blithesome Jennie,
Light of heart and bright of eye;
None that see thee, of the many,
Can thy wealth of charms deny.
Light and airy
As a fairy,
Flitting down the rural lane;
Sunshine bringing,
Always singing!
Loving, cheerful, joyous Jane.

IDEALITY.

The beauty of the faith in goodness,
The beauty of the power that moulds,
And shapes, and fits our forms and beings
To fitting palaces for souls;
The beauty of a lofty purpose,
That which inspires to better things,
Pointing aloft, and to the morning
Which, full of promise, upward springs.

The power that rules the lives of mortals,
Stamps there an image all its own;
The ruling power, whate'er its purpose,
Erects, and sits upon its throne.
To wisely choose for self a ruler
Who shall from error set us free,
Is man's most earnest, solemn duty —
Far reaching as eternity.

ALONE.

Alone! no home or loved ones near;
  All day the storm-clouds fill the air,
And Summer's brightest skies are drear;
  All thoughts are thoughts of dark despair,
E'en laughter dieth in the moan—
              Alone, alone.

Alone! and yet the careless throng
  Surges about me, and the hum
Of constant voices heard in song,
  Drum on my ear which seemeth dumb,
Or hears in every sound the groan—
              Alone, alone.

Alone! how heavy on the heart
  The sense of desolation falls!
Before it all life's joys depart,
  As memory the past recalls:
Grim skeletons of joys long flown—
              Alone, alone.

TURNING OF THE TIDE.

Now calm I lie dreaming,
    Stretched out on my bed,
Alive, yet half seeming,
    As though I were dead.

The fever receding,
    Yet haunting my brain,
As though but conceding
    One-half of its reign.

Or, like some exulting,
    And murderous foe,
As though but consulting
    The finishing blow.

To see loved forms gliding,
    Like spirits about
My bed, or abiding
    Near to me in doubt.

Looking so feelingly
Down into my face,
And so appealingly,
As if hope to trace.

Then all so tearfully
They turn from my bed,
Sobbing so fearfully,
Oft thinking me dead.

And yet to be living,
And know all around,
Yet powerless of giving
A sign or a sound.

I fear no disaster,
Though scarce have I breath:
I know I shall master
This skeleton — death.

At length I grow weary,
I sink quite away;
I hear not the query:
"How is he, to-day?"

At last I awaken,
Refreshed, without pain;
My strength I've mistaken.
I slumber again.

And now I lie resting,
So sweet in my bed,
And know I am besting
The foe we all dread.

A MYSTERY.

I wonder: Was Time ever young?
Had he a birth — a golden morn?
Who round his infant cradle sung?
From whence his life, if he were born?
If he were born, then he must die —
His death would mark eternity;
Who o'er his grave would grieve or sigh?
Ah, well; how deep the mystery!

LOVING AND FISHING.

On a lovely Autumn morning,
  I and lovely Bessie Lee
Listened to the boatman's warning
  And went fishing on the sea;
Went a-rocking on the billows,
  Which were rolling to and fro,
Like the golden weeping willows
  When the winds their branches blow;
Where the great waves were a-snapping
  As they came a-near the land —
Bessie said "their hands were clapping
  'Cause they'd reached the golden sand."

It then seemed they were rejoicing
  Over something of the kind,
For their mellow, muffled voicing
  Spoke of pleasure to my mind.
All the air seemed filled with singing,
  And it seemed that I could see
Water-nymphs and mermaids ringing
  Silver bells beneath the sea;
And the music there, in dying,
  Fell so sweetly on our ears
That our souls were moved to sighing,
  And our eyes were moist with tears.

Then I tried to speak; said something
  About the weather and the wave,
But Bessie, silent, answered nothing,
  Save for nodding, low and grave,
To my mention of the beauty
  Which was in the tossing sea,
And of that sweet, solemn duty —
  Worshiping of melody.
Presently she asked a story,
  And I cleared my throat to tell
That old tale, so full of glory —
  Sweeter than the sound of bell.

WATER-NYMPHS AND MERMAIDS RINGING
SILVER BELLS BENEATH THE SEA.

UNIV. OF
CALIFORNIA

But my heart was quite unsteady,
  Like our boat upon the wave,
And I found I was not ready
  All to lose, or all to save.
I have heard of some great master,
  Who'd his life work almost done,
One more stroke: would dire disaster
  Follow this most fateful one?
It had been so with our loving,
  Courting most by look and hand;
Would my speaking be the proving
  For our hearts no golden sand?

And that question kept on rising,
  As a cloud obscured my mind,
Until it was not surprising
  That I faltered, halt and blind;
For it seemed like hope was sinking
  Deep and deeper in the sea,
Doubt and fear, together linking,
  Joined to chain and fetter me;
Till that girl — oh, Heaven bless her! —
  Came and sat close by my side,
And with fond looks bade me kiss her —
  Loving seal of promised bride.

Teardrops glistened on her lashes,
  As her head so sweetly lay
On my bosom, and their flashes
  Of love's jewels made display.
Peaceful, quiet, solemn, tender,
  Was the light from those dear eyes,
All so sweet that I would render
  Every tribute 'neath the skies.
Every thought filled with devotion,
  Set to wondrous melody,
As, with tenderest emotion,
  We found Love's treasure-trove at sea.

All unnoticed were surroundings,
All to each, whate'er betide;
In the sea of Love, the soundings
Are unmeasured, as we glide
Ever onward, on forever,
Safe while Cupid mans the oar,
For his piloting has never
Wrecked a bark upon the shore;
Straight he guides our little vessel
To an inlet where the land
Forms a harbor where we nestle
Safely on the golden sand.

There, hand-clasped, we sat and listened
To the music of the sea,
As the sunlight danced and glistened
To its ceaseless melody.
"We came fishing," said she blushing,
"Will our baskets never fill?"
"Never while our hearts are rushing
To obey King Cupid's will."
So we sat there until even
Cast its shadows o'er the land,
Catching glimpses straight from Heaven
Gleaming on the golden sand.

THE COQUETTE.

Jaunty, willful, debonair,
Bright and handsome, passing fair,
Tripping a-down the street;
Catching hearts within her hair
To tread beneath her feet.

WHY?

Why battle with Fate and in feebleness cry?
"Eat, drink and be merry, to-morrow ye die."

Ye cannot check Time, he will ever roll on,
And death will pursue thee, as evening the dawn.

Aye, Death will o'ertake thee, whatever thy course,
The present is thine for the better or worse.

The present: how little, and yet it is all,
From cradle of flowers, to the hearse and the pall.

We live but by moments: life is but the *now;*
The future for thee may no grace yet allow.

Be like the poor moth-wing: be fooled with the flame;
It is true to its nature: Who is to blame?

The bee seeks for honey, the wolf for its prey;
The owl loves the night-time far better than day.

All life lives on other life, 'til in its turn,
It falls in the swirl of Time's all-grinding urn.

Up with the daylight and gather the flowers;
The jewels of life are its bright, sunny hours.

If you love the blossoms, then cull them to keep,
For Winter will soon o'er the flower kingdom sweep.

Be dull as the sloth, or as serpents be wise;
He gives to the one and the other denies.

Whatever ye are in a measure is true
To the lottery card which at birth-time ye drew.

Why battle with Fate and in feebleness cry?
"Eat, drink and be merry, to-morrow ye die."

COME, LOVE, AND SPEAK.

Come, Love, and speak!
What shall you say? Speak from your soul to me
Of all those sweeter thoughts that fill thy heart,
And make for me the heaven that thou art;
For as the thirsty sky draws from the sea
The cooling mists for it to feed upon,
So is thy tender touch, thy voice and smile,
To the parched desert of my life, where gone
Is every flower, save one, me to beguile —
Without thy presence I am lone and weak,
Come, Love, and speak.

Come, Love, and speak!
I cannot bear this silence longer, dear;
I have no heart for aught on earth, but thee.
Whence come these troubling shades of doubt and fear,
And muffled sobbings, like the restless sea?
Calling unto the life of all the earth
To now return and sleep within her breast,
From whence they sprang, at kiss of sun, to birth;
So doth my soul call unto thine for rest,
And will thus evermore thy true love seek:
Come, Love, and speak!

TO A CHILD.

Sweet child of joy, if it could be,
That to thee, in the future years,
No storms would come and angrily
Becloud thy life with sorrow's tears,
I would not counsel thee to-day,
That life cannot be always May.

The rose thou thinkest now so sweet,
Will soon reveal its piercing thorn;
All joys have wings, of motion fleet,
As rosy tintings of the morn,
For in the heated hours of day,
Life's burdens rest full heavily.

After the Spring of joy and bloom,
There cometh frosts of pain and care;
Joys, with the flowers, fall to the tomb,
And death-damps fill the Autumn air,
While Winter's breath across the wold,
Flecks all earth's garments with the mold.

I would but speak to warn thee now,
That in the future there will be
A crown of thorns for every brow,
That guards not well its purity;
Preserve this jewel through the strife,
And thou shalt win the crown of life.

TO VIOLET.

I dream of thee, I dream of thee,
My sweet and lovely Violet;
Waking, sleeping, thy face I see,
Nor one sweet charm do I forget.
Thy gentle sigh, thy melting tear,
Thy trusting hope and trembling fear,
Thy loving tone when I am near,
Are ever with me, Violet.

No sweeter charm can ever come
To mortal man, my Violet,
Though through elysian fields he roam,
Than comes to me, my gentle pet,
As I recount each moment o'er,
And every new one add'st the store,
A sweeter than I knew before
I met thee, charming Violet.

Joy of my heart! Soul of my life!
My priceless treasure, Violet;
Wilt thou not be my own dear wife?
And if thou wilt, thou'lt ne'er regret
The day that makest thee my own;
For "'Tis not good man be alone,
Nor lonely be," in sweetest tone,
Whispered my own, sweet Violet.

TO AN ABSENT LOVE.

Oh, could you know the weary hours
  I've spent since last I heard from thee,
How pains my heart, how throbs my head,
  How all my life is misery,
You'd hasten then to speak your love,
  To soothe my brow and ease my pain;
Be true, oh! darling, to yourself,
  And speak those words of love again.

Speak frankly, let no shade of doubt
  Lurk in the words that tell my fate;
Speak truly, though the truth should leave
  My heart all crushed and desolate.
For Love doth live on trust and truth
  And cycles of eternal years
Doth frost not its immortal youth,
  Though bathed in sorrows and in tears.

FRIENDSHIP.

To one and all within this hall,
  I fill this sparkling cup;
Drink to the toast, I love the most,
  And drain it every drop!
It is the toast of friendship true,
  Of life the brightest gem,
I here and now would offer you—
  Earth's purest diadem.

The chain which binds all noble minds,
  In love and unity;
Matchless its strength—endless its length,
  Reaching o'er land and sea.
Then let us drink to friendship true,
  The priceless, peerless gem,
Exemplified by Him who rose,
  As star of Bethlehem.

CALMING THE STORM.

Rejoice, all ye people! in harmony raise
  Your voice to the Lord in one mighty acclaim;
Let heaven's blue arches resound with the praise,
  You joyfully render unto His great name.

The Lord has been with us in wonderful power,
  And wrong from his temples again has been hurl'd,
And right wields the wand of command in this hour,
  While liberty blossoms all over the world.

Rejoice, for the powerful Goliah is slain;
  Rejoice, for his slaves are unhanded and free!
Oh, sweet was the music, as falling, their chains
  Struck the chords which awoke the world's jubilee!

Purified by the fire of war's with'ring flame,
  Which rolled like a raging sea over our form,
When Peace from the clouds of the hurricane came—
  The voice of Divinity calming the storm.

A TOAST AT A BANQUET.

I.

Fill up the goblets; a toast to Queen Pleasure!
  Life without wine, for this hour, is too slow;
All fill them, with me, then tread we a measure,
  Improving the moments, as swiftly they go.
Light is the heart, while with joyousness dizzy;
  Bright is the eye, while the lips form a smile;
With merriment now we all should be busy,
  Fill up the goblets! we'll mourn afterwhile.

II.

Fill up the goblets and clink them together!
  Fill to the brim with the bright ruby wine;
Heed not the season; who cares for foul weather?
  Joy is of life the sweet crown all divine.
On with the music, so richly entrancing;
  The jewels of life to us all now belong;
On with the story, the quaffing and dancing;
  Joy's trinity's here: wine, women and song!

On the Death of a Lady.

Rest well sweet flower;
The lives of all about thee here
Were by thy spirit rendered bright;
To such as thou the way is clear,
No shadows make for thee a night;
Rest well, sweet flower,
Death brings to thee but greater power.

Sweet spirit, rest,
Thy life was one fair, fragrant bloom,
Each year a rose of spotless white;
The petals fall into the tomb,
The fragrance lives, and yields delight,
The world to bless
With its sweet power of gentleness.

Thou art not here,
And yet methinks I hear thee speak
In each soft breeze, in each bright flower,
To all the faint, and bid them seek
Strength from the fount of matchless power;
And thus art here,
The weak to guide, the faint to cheer.

A true, white rose,
So purely sweet, so sweetly pure,
All hearts to thee in love incline;
Thy power for aye shall yet endure,
Death cannot break a thought divine.
Rest well, sweet rose,
Eternal bliss be thy repose.

MY CREED.

We are, and may before have been,
May in the future be;
'Tis all the finite mind can know,
All else is mystery.

BURY OUR LOVE?

Bury our love! Was that what you said?
  Blot the bright star of hope out of our sky;
Wreck each of our lives on the threshold of joy;
  Starve each of our souls till they wither and die!

Hang our harps on the willows, ne'er more to tune them!
  Still the sweet song of love, ere its best notes be sung!
Draw the black pall of night o'er life's day of rejoicing,
  When its golden-hued morning has only begun?

Blight the opening bud, ere it blooms forth in beauty?
  Turn to ashes the rose, and destroy its perfume?
Strip the sweet tree of life of all of its pleasures,
  And leave not a bud on its branches to bloom?

Pluck not the rich fruit, when 'tis matured and full ripened?
  When first 'tis expressed, decline the rich wine?
When the feast is prepared and the guests all assembled,
  Refuse on its richness and sweetness to dine?

When the heart and the soul combine in their pleading,
  To be fed on the richness and sweetness of love,
Oh, list to their voices, and heed their entreating;
  Then the earth will be like unto heaven above!

The harvest is ripe and the roses are blooming,
  Thy sweet smiles were their sun, and thy tears were their dew;
They've grown and are ripened for thee, my sweet darling,
  And can only be gathered and garnered by you.

DARLING WILMA.

Angels called our little treasure
  To a home beyond the sky,
Robbed us of our dearest pleasure,
  And we vainly ask them why?
Has she gone, alas! forever?
  Sorrow's tears they fall like rain;
Darling Wilma, will she never—
  Never to us speak again?

DARLING WILMA.

See the work of Death's cold finger
Round her beauteous lips and eyes,
Half concealing smiles that linger —
A sweetness that e'en Death defies.
Are they closed, alas! forever?
Oh, the load of bitter pain!
Will her brown eyes on us never —
Never on us look again?

Baby's clasp, how sweet and tender,
As her arms around us twine,
And to heaven the praise we render
For this precious gift divine.
Are they cold, alas! forever?
Will we feel no more their strain?
Will her dear arms clasp us never —
Never clasp our necks again?

Baby's ruby lips, how loving!
Like the rosebuds of the Spring,
Ever music sweet unfolding,
Like the songs the angels sing.
Are they silent, cold forever?
At the thought how burns the brain!
Will her sweet lips kiss us never —
Never kiss our lips again?

Hope beyond Death's shining river
Beams upon us from afar,
With the promise of the Giver
Of the light to every star.
Glorious star that shines forever!
Shines for all in doubt and pain;
There, beyond Death's welcome river,
We shall meet our child again.

A VISION.

I.

In youth I saw a vision, wondrous fair;
The clouds within the sky did shape themselves
Like unto one vast, gorgeous gallery;
And, from all points around, there winging came
Ten thousand harpers, with their harps of gold.
And, presently, the brilliant air was filled
With notes of sweetest melody and song,
Which floated out upon the balmy air
And fell upon my ear with soothing sound.

II.

And I beheld a parting in the clouds,
Through which, familiar to my eyes, a form
Appeared, with snowy robe and harp of gold.
Then did the sweet winds, breathing faint, yet clear,
Come to my ear again, wafting a song
Such as no mortal ear e'er heard before;
It was a song of joy and praise divine,
Bringing a balm for sorrow in each sound.
Lo! through the parting in the clouds, there came
A flood of dazzling light, which reached to Heaven,
Up which the white-robed harpers disappeared,
Chanting an anthem grand, the notes of which
Still echo in my soul, making this life
More bright for this sweet vision's having been.

WRITTEN IN A YOUNG LADY'S ALBUM.

Sweet maiden, rich in Nature's grace,
With eyes of brown and raven hair,
May Sorrow's shade ne'er cloud thy face,
Nor pale thy rosy lips with care.

Time those jet locks will turn to gray,
But Love's sweet, gentle, soothing art
Hath power to drive all gloom away,
And youth preserve within thy heart.

ADDRESS TO DEATH.

'Tis I you want this time, Old Boy?
Well, I am ready now to go;
Bring you me peace, or pain, or joy?
Go I above or down below?

Come now, Old Fellow, tell me, pray,
What doth the Future hold for me?
Which is the straight and narrow way?—
I've asked of everyone but thee.

Some men have said: This is the road,
And others said 'twas surely that;
Go which I would, Life's galling load
Upon my shoulders heavy sat.

And thou wilt lift it — let me rest?
Ah, Death, thou surely art my friend;
And I will deem thee kindest, best,
If thou of Life prove but the end.

TULIPS.

I do declare a form more fair
It never was my chance to meet,
Than maid with wealth of golden hair,
Who tends the flowers across the street.
The violets are in her eyes,
And on her cheek the roses bloom,
And in her smile a charm there lies
Which drives away all thought of gloom.
And never did such tulips grow,
So rich and loving and so sweet;
I would their sweetness I might know,
And my two lips her two lips greet!

GOLDEN HAIR.

I saw in dreams a maiden fair,
Whose smile was all that love could know;
A golden banner was her hair,
Which rose and fell in radiant flow;
Emblem of her true character.

I know I've had my hours of fun,
From many flowers have sipped the dew,
None have allowed at waste to run —
The joys of life I've missed are few.

But then, what's of it, when 'tis done?
At best a merry holiday;
Not much the "pot" when it you've won —
For life I care not here to stay.

So, if you're ready, pack your grip,
And let's be going: I'll not sigh;
I'm ready now to take the trip.
Old world of trouble, bye-you-bye.

WHAT IS DEATH?

You think him dead? let me whisper, dear,
This one sweet thought to your listening ear:
God never made a being so grand,
Just to blot it out, you understand.

He could not cause these tears to flow,
And cloud your life with deepest woe,
And sear your heart with bitter pain,
And torture thus your weary brain.

The star of hope he would not place,
Within the heart of all the race,
If he held not in goodly store,
The lives of those who've gone before.

This quenchless hope He would not give,
If human souls e'er cease to live:
A burning thirst, an arid sky,
And waters none to them supply,

Would wisdom be, and mercy, too,
Compared to this, if I and you
For our hungry souls shall have no bread?
Then better far that we were dead;

Or, better still, that we ne'er had been,
Of this world a part, with its pain and sin.
But 'tis not so: no want is known,
From God's green foot-stool to His throne.

But He has placed, with tender care,
The means of satisfaction there.
He feeds the ravens when they cry,
A sparrow's fall is not passed by.

Then think you, dear, the highest goal,
To which turns every human soul,
Is but a myth within the air?
Believe it not: thy love is there.

TO A BEAUTIFUL MAIDEN.

They told me you were beautiful;
That deep within your lustrous eyes
The Summer's sunlight never dies;
That clearly on your dear, sweet face
Were constantly portrayed each grace,
And that your soft and silken hair
Was like to that the angels wear;
That your soft, dimpled cheeks, so fair,
Had caught Morn's blush and held it there.

But, oh! the rapturous delight
Which thrilled my soul at the first sight
Of your angelic loveliness,
Was purest type of mortal bliss!
Eye hath not seen, brush cannot paint,
So fair, so pure, so sweet a saint;
Embodiment, unto my mind,
Of all that's best of human kind.

THE SEA OF GALILEE.

Cradled among thy low-browed hills,
  Which stand around like sentinels;
Enraptured thought my bosom fills,
  While on thy shores my fancy dwells.

For here the man-God dwelt and taught,
  Upon thy shores, oh, sacred sea;
That wondrous, solemn, peaceful thought,
  Sweet thought of immortality!

The gentle winds from off thy breast
  Seem pure and sacred to me now;
They by His presence have been blest,
  Have cooled the Holy Savior's brow.

When worn and weary, weak and faint,
  Have lulled to rest and sweet repose,
The God in man, the kingly saint,
  Who lived and died for others' woes.

Therefore, oh sea, I love thy shores,
  Thy arid, scorched and burning sands
My thankful heart this spot adores
  Above all other earthly lands.

SOURCE OF CONSOLATION.

Oh, where for comfort should we go,
Dear Lord, except to thee,
When waves of sorrow swiftly flow
Upon us like a sea?

When all the sunshine of our life
Is drowned in chilling rain,
And bitter is the weary strife
And hoping seems in vain?

When earthly friends grow formal, cold,
And pass us proudly by;
When we are helpless, sick and old,
And Pleasure's fount is dry?

Oh! could we bear, dear Lord, to live,
Or who would dare to die,
Did not Thy loving spirit give
Us comfort from on high?

Did not thy loving spirit say:
"Come, weary, wandering child,
And dwell in realms of endless day,
Pure, stainless, undefiled?"

Thy hand can chase all grief away,
Thy spirit ease each pain;
To each believing heart dost say:
"Though dead, ye live again."

HER GRAVE.

O'er her grave the nightingale sings,
And the soft breeze sigheth low,
As day departs on golden wings,
And night her sable mantle flings,
Over all the world below.
Then the stars with golden light,
Pierce the curtains of the night,
And watch beside her lonely grave,
O'er which the willow branches wave.

DESPONDENCY.

There are times in life when living seems one ceaseless, bitter pain;
When from the cold, gray clouds above us falls, incessantly, the rain,
And the morning and the evening brings to us no light again.

When our Junes are all Decembers, cold their light and chill their breeze,
And no prospect, in our vision, brings a thought our hearts to please,
And the troubles of the moment banish every sense of ease.

When we feel a tender sorrow, walking ever by our side,
Dim and gaunt the shadows swiftly ever by us onward glide,
And we feel our courage ebbing—ebbing slowly with the tide.

THE OUTCAST.

Though golden streams of sunlight pour,
About my daily path,
I hear alone the tempest roar,
The hurricane's fierce wrath!

Storm tossed upon a raging sea,
A starless sky o'erhead;
There is no ray of hope for me,
All peace and light have fled.

For me of life there is no June;
December's chilling breath,
With hungry stars and waning moon,
Are mine, always, 'til death.

But death! how sweeps the wild despair
At thought of shroud and pall;
Deep darkness fills the very air—
Death ends not, is not all!

There is one hope: one hope for me!
'Tis He who stilled the wave,
When raging ran the stormy sea:
Who said: "Come, I will save!"

EXPERIENCE.

Mother, I find that the pleasures of this life depart with its morn,
Like the fresh and pearly dewdrops that bejewel the blades of corn;
Like mists that hang o'er the river, and hood the great mountains and hills,
Then away to the great, blue air-sea, then back to the lakes and rills.

Only, our pleasures return not, when once from our lives they have flown;
Once gone, they are gone forever, and never more will they return.
I find this loving and hating, and hating and loving again,
Brings less of joy than of sadness, and far less of pleasure than pain.

MY OTHER SELF.

This other self of myself, do you know,
Is a demon black of the fiends of hell;
Hist! whisper it low, curst thought more low.
Why ring it out with a clarion bell?

This evil wretch I have known all my days,
He has dogged my steps since my life begun,
Throwing his shadows over all my ways,
Malignant and black as a skeleton.

I smile and laugh, but beneath it there lies
This fiendish form of malignant hate;
All thoughts of virtue and truth he derides,
And steadily drags me down to my fate.

He has made me crush full many a flower,
And sneer at virtue I could not attain:
He holds my life in the grasp of his power,
And swears me no respite while life shall remain.

'Tis well he keeps well away when I feel
The bitter dregs he has caused me to drink,
Or I'd grind his head 'neath an iron heel,
Or to the depths of hell I'd with him sink.

Some time, some place, we two surely will clash,
And the end will come, if it end in death;
I've promised myself to do nothing rash,
But I'll fight this fiend while I've strength and breath.

I'll see him suffer, though my soul be damned
    To the lowest depths of a burning hell;
I'd torture him slow, while my fierceness calmed,
    To a level lower than Satan fell.

Oh, God! how I wish he were flesh and blood,
    That I could but place him upon the rack,
And poison his veins till the crimson flood
    Would be lit with a flame which would not slack!

I think that nothing would please me more
    Than to grasp his throat with a clasp of hate,
And grip till the blood from his every pore
    Should, drop by drop, slowly measure his fate.

To turn the wheel slowly, his limbs to stretch,
    Till Pain should limnings of agony trace
More horribly still, on the soulless wretch,
    While I should mockingly laugh in his face.

AN OCEAN GRAVE.

Oh, ocean deep, thy vigils keep
    Above her lonely grave;
Forever mourn, forever weep,
    And kiss her with each wave.

Lull her to rest within thy breast,
    Sing to her soft and low;
When daylight fades dim in the West
    Let fresh winds sweetly blow.

And they shall bring, on tireless wing,
    A sigh, a prayer, a tear,
From one whose constant suffering
    Ends not while waiting here.

For one whose breath, 'til kindly death
    Shall call his spirit hence,
Will waft a prayer on every breath,
    To do her reverence.

THE PAST.

Though still and dead,
My soul is wed
To thoughts and scenes of other years;
My early youth
I love, forsooth,
For its sweet innocence and truth,
Far better than my later years.

Its shadowy hills,
Its pleasant rills,
Its meadows fresh, and gardens fair,
Undimmed I see,
As then, so free,
I wandered o'er the grassy lea
And breathed their fresh and fragrant air.

I love to walk
Again, and talk,
By memory's aid, beneath the trees;
To list again
Down in the glen,
Where in my youth I've often been,
To mystic tale of evening breeze.

TO A FADED FLOWER.

Dear, faded flower, there lingers yet,
About thy leaves a rare perfume,
More sweet than rose or violet,
Doth e'er exhale in fairest bloom.

For, ere she gave me thee, sweet flower,
She plucked thee from her bosom fair;
Where thou lay blushing for an hour,
And breathing sweetness on the air.

She pressed thee to her lips, my flower,
And hallowed thee with fondest kiss;
Earth holdeth not within her power,
A purer, richer gift than this.

My precious flower, dear, faded flower,
Thou hast been honored, richly blessed:
Hast lain upon her breast an hour,
By her sweet lips hast been caressed!

ETERNITY.

Eternity! Eternity!
From the beginning to the end;
How rolls the echo back to me,
Like sobbings of some unknown sea,
O'er which our weary pathways tend!

Eternity! it cannot be,
That aught but truth shall e'er endure;
That sin shall roll unfettered, free,
An angry, stern, relentless sea,
To toss and wreck the good and pure.

Eternity! oh, God, how long!
Boundless, unmeasured, and unknown!
Above, beyond the human throng;
To thee alone doth power belong,
To compass all unto thy throne.

When all the worlds were formless, void,
Eternity rolled back through space,
And far beyond the spoken word,
When none thy voice's echo heard,
Stood emblem of thy matchless grace.

A QUESTION.

The forever of the future,
The forever of the past,
The forever changing present,
Will they all forever last?
We, the foam upon the ocean,
The mere product of the motion
Of the forces which create,
Could we measure all the forces,
In their devious, winding courses,
We might solve our future state.

MY QUEEN.

Soft violets blossom in her eyes,
And on her cheek the tint of roses,
While in her heart there hidden lies
A Cupid sweet, her smile discloses.

THE PROPHESY.

Awake, oh, ye sleepers! the flood gates are swinging,
And high roll the billows and swift runs the tide;
The oncoming years a Marseillaise are singing,
A great revolution is fast spreading wide!
Awake! oh, ye sleepers! and climb to the summit
Of prophesy's mountain, and take a survey:
The future demands that the square and the plummet
Shall measurements take, which the world must obey.

Awake! oh, ye sleepers! for just indignation,
Shall sweep like a flood of destruction along,
Destroying the evil and cleansing the Nation,
From crimes which arise from consenting to wrong!
Then woe to the wicked and wretched despoiler,
Whose vile work is the ruin of his fellow men;
Who steals from the trembling hand of the toiler—
'Twould be better for him that he never had been!

Then woe to the party that panders to passion;
That treads out the voice of the conscience and heart;
That revels alone in the power of possession;
That bids not its errors in haste to depart!
The sun of its triumph is fast near its setting;
The light of its glory is fading away;
The heart of the people rebel at abetting,
The crimes that are cursing the Nation today.

THE OLD HOMESTEAD.

Nothing here lingers;
Time's restless fingers
The scene have changed and altered all,
Memory endears,
Of other years,
And covered them as with a pall.

All here is strange,
Oh, such a change,
Old time has wrought by flight of years!
Many are dead,
And all are wed,
To later life of joy or tears.

Those who were strong,
Have passed along,
Life's river till their strength is passed;
A few more days,
Of Summer haze,
And there life's sun will shed its last.

Soon they will be
At liberty,
For soon the welcome gate of death,
Will open wide,
And 'neath the tide
Of Time they'll yield their mortal breath.

Alas! 'tis dead—
The life I knew,
With youth's bright, joyous hours has fled;
The false, the true,
Like morning dew,
Has flown and left a chill of dread!

LADY BROWN.

Clear, honest eyes has Lady Brown;
  Such soulful eyes! You feel them speak
  Whene'er her looks your glances seek;
Those eyes have won a great renown
          For Lady Brown.

She wears a coat, does Lady Brown,
  As soft as silk, with airs as grand
  As any lady in the land;
Polished and fine, from tip to crown,
          Is Lady Brown.

If she should speak, should Lady Brown,
  She could not tell of Noah's ark;
  She could at best but whine or bark.
But then, she knows a smile or frown,
          Does Lady Brown.

When I lay sick, this Lady Brown
Would come and sit beside my bed,
With looks as plain as though words said:
"Shall I not run the stairway down
For Colonel Brown?"

A wave of hand, and Lady Brown
Would, instantly, walk swift away,
And by her looks and actions say:
"Colonel, for you I just came down"—
Would Lady Brown.

Thoughtful and kind was Lady Brown;
Whenever I was sound asleep
She'd softly through my chamber creep,
Or, 'til I wakened, lay her down,
Would Lady Brown.

WHATEVER YOU WILL.

This world is whatsoe'er they wish
To every being in it;
The good or bad
Can e'er be had,
On call, at any minute.

And every one may take his will,
And have it to the letter;
But raise his voice,
Pronounce his choice,
For ill, or good, or better.

Like unto like will surely cleave,
Be whatsoe'er the station:
Moths to the night,
Birds to the light,
All over God's creation.

The humming bird will love the rose;
The vulture has its feature:
The sly fox knows
His safe repose,
Likewise each other creature.

The low, the vicious, and the vile,
Will seek their chosen level;
Will be as one
While rolls the sun,
And all go to the devil.

But, thank the Lord, those who may choose
The pathway of transition,
May reach the goal
Of the pure soul
That loves Heaven's condition.

THE TIRELESS SHIP.

This old world ships a motley crew,
For its swift voyage round the sun;
About its shoreless sea of blue,
How the old ship doth haste to run!

Bounding away day after day,
Without a shroud, or sail, or spar;
It speeds along its beaten way,
Nor ever stops, its force to mar.

It is as grain of sand to shore —
A fragment of some greater thing,
Tossed out in space to roll before
The wave of that one's greater wing.

And pigmies scamper o'er its deck,
Or walk sedately here and there;
As though their will could save from wreck,
Or swerve its course a single hair.

A pigmy, thinking him a king,
And guiding the old world to port,
Proves him a pigmy without wing,
And fit with every fool to sport.

Each insect of the earth, though small,
Feels its importance, just the same;
And each to each, alike to all,
Confers the honor(?) of a name!

VENICE.

I stand within thy sea-girt bounds,
And listen to thy mystic sounds
As from the deeper, farther sea,
They come with fairy songs to thee,
Bearing upon each crested wave
The secrets of some hidden cave.

Resting in peace upon the sea,
Beautiful queen of Italy,
Thou art a vision, oh, so fair!
With sparkling waters for each street,
Which lave and kiss thy mossy feet
And cool thy soft and fragrant air.

A TWILIGHT MEMORY.

When dying day, with softened grace,
The shadows of the twilight trace
Across the bosom of the earth,
Then in the gloaming come to me,
From out the halls of memory,
Visions of her who gave love birth.

I see love dancing in her eyes,
And on her lips in sweetness lies
The darling impulse of her heart;
And trembling o'er her fair, young form,
Love's crimson blushes, pure and warm,
Spring from the wounds of Cupid's dart.

Then every glance, so sweet and shy,
Is clear to my adoring eye,
As when those brown eyes sparkling sent
Her youthful soul, so pure and sweet,
Upon its mission mine to greet
With love's expressive sentiment.

THE HAUNTED LAKE.

There's a deep, blue lake that's haunted,
And the bravest and undaunted
Never yet a sail have flaunted
  To the wind which o'er it rolls;
For though it may have the seeming
Of a placid, peaceful dreaming,
Yet its waves are ever teeming
  With a legion of lost souls.

Many years — they are unnumbered —
Since it has thus peaceful slumbered,
Since it has been unincumbered
  By the flutter of a sail;
When a band of merry-makers
Ploughed its bosom — echo-wakers,
Shouting loud, 'til 'neath its breakers
  They sank down with sob and wail.

And, they say, so runs the story
Of this dark *memento mori*,
Falling from the aged and hoary,
  That a maiden, young and fair
Saw a Siren in the water,
Who imploringly besought her
To become her loving daughter,
  From the regions of the air.

And this Siren sang so sweetly
That she charmed the maid completely;
And the maiden dived so neatly
  'Neath the gently swelling wave,
That her comrades were confounded,
And so greatly were astounded,
That their lips no murmur sounded,
  As they looked upon her grave.

There they waited, speechless, seeming
As if paralyzed or dreaming,
Where the water-lilies, teeming.
    Spread their palms upon the lake;
Waiting for the maid's returning,
With their anxious hearts all yearning,
And their throbbing temples burning
    With a flame that would not slake.

Then a low wind softly winging
O'er the waters came, there bringing
Sound of myriad voices singing;
    And the waters rose and fell
As if demons, fierce in motion,
Had the lake changed to an ocean,
Whose wild, frantic, fierce commotion
    Grew more powerful with each swell.

Then the billows rose, and dashing
That frail barque sent trembling, crashing
Hither, thither, yonder, lashing,
    'Til all sank with shriek and groan;
Then the waters in their madness
Seemed to shout in tones of gladness,
Which they sudden changed to sadness —
    Which has since then been their tone.

Since that day all barques have warning,
From the gloaming 'til the morning,
None will think the tale of scorning;
    Hence upon this haunted lake
Never oar nor sail appeareth,
For all sailors greatly feareth
That if they a barque there steereth,
That the demons will awake.

DREAMING.

I would I might forever dream,
    For waking hours are full of woe,
As drops of water in the stream
    That never cease to onward flow.

AN ANGEL'S VISIT.

Heaven sent to our home a dear little stranger,
A sweet, blue-eyed darling, with soft, sunny hair,
As pure as the God-child that lay in the manger,
Was this, our own darling, our beautiful heir.

Then our sweet cup of joy was filled to o'erflowing,
Each morning of life seemed more fresh and more fair,
And Heaven itself seemed enriched by bestowing
Upon us this flower from its garden so fair.

LIFE'S LESSON.

My star of hope sinks in a cloud of gloom,
I vainly struggle 'gainst the tide of fate;
Nothing is certain but the gaping tomb,
To which I drift all lone and desolate.

Life's burden groweth heavy with the years;
The present doth the past alone repeat;
Its bitter sorrows, poignant grief and tears
Doth beat upon and tread me 'neath their feet.

The cruel darts of sorrow pierce my soul,
And grief with heavy curtains drapes my heart;
Remorse in heavy waves doth o'er me roll,
And long I this life's troubles to depart.

Pleasure is but a blank, unmarked by pain,
An idle eddy in the stream of life,
Where we may list unto some sweet refrain
Between the battles of this weary strife.

The oil of rich desire now burneth low,
The fruits that once were sweet now bitter seem;
E'en Hope has lost the power she used to know,
And flickers faintly her once radiant gleam.

This is the lesson all must come to learn;
The crucial test of character and will
Is that which makes the soul and heart to burn,
'Til all dross be consumed, that peace may fill.

A MAGICAL CITY.

Far up in a maze of glory
    By omnipotence uphurled,
Tower the domes, and spires, and steeples
    Of a grand and silent world.

Far above the noise and bustle
    Of the rushing feet below,
Are the towering, cloud-capped mountains,
    With their coronets of snow.

When the light of day has left us,
    And the mantle of the night
Is enfolding us in silence,
    All those peaks are bathed in light.

There the sunbeams love to linger,
    Kissing beauty into birth,
And to crown with flames of glory
    All those snow-wreathed kings of earth.

Like some splendid, radiant city
    To my rapturous gaze they seem,
All illuminated grandly
    By the day-god's golden gleam.

And methinks I oft hear music
    Falling to the world below,
From the lutes of mountain spirits
    In those palaces of snow.

And I sometimes weep in sadness,
    For this music sweet I know
Will fade like a dream of beauty ;
    Will melt like the flakes of snow.

And my soul cries out in anguish
    That this scene should fade and die,
And the low winds in the gloaming
    Echo back my lonely cry.

ON KISSING.

My Rose, few know the wondrous bliss,
The sweet, ecstatic thrill,
When all the soul within a kiss
Is given with a will;
And yet with that soft, gentle touch,
Which speaks of passion not too much.

Come, love, while shadows fold the hour,
And sit beside me here,
While Nature, with her silent power,
Our hearts to each endear;
And let us with affection kiss,
Our hearts to love's unmeasured bliss.

WITHOUT AND WITHIN.

To and fro,
To and fro,
The willows sway amid the storm;
The raindrops clash,
And wildly dash
Against the window pane and sash,
While all within is light and warm.

QUEEN OF THE MUSES.

My own loved queen, forever reign
With undisputed sway,
And to my heart love's glad refrain
Repeat from day to day;
And when the shadows of the night
Remove the day's bright beam,
Fill thou my soul with sweet delight,
By love's enchanting dream.

SUNSET.

The sun has passed from the mountain,
  And thrown his last kiss to the sea ;
The spray from the splashing fountain
  No longer bediamonds the lea.
The king of day has departed
  With his gorgeously brilliant train ;
The world is wrapped in night's curtain,
  'Til day's glorious coming again.

The toil, the sorrow, the weeping,
  The blasting and withering pain,
Gives way to the peaceful creeping
  Of comforting sleep o'er the brain.
A sweet and comforting message
  Comes from immortality's plain,
Its sweet-scented, life-giving breezes
  My sad soul exultingly seizes,
And I fear no more the dark river,
  The blood-chilling, life-killing river,
For I shall reach Heaven's bright plain,
  Kind Heaven's soul's home-prepared plain.

I feel my journey is ended,
  My beacon-light dies in the West ;
My day with night's gloaming is blended,
  I calmly lie down to my rest,
As a child on its mothers breast sleeping,
  The innocent sleep of the blest.
As the winds from the lethean river
  A song sweetly sing to my soul —
A lullaby sing to my soul,
  And my spirit goes up to life's Giver,
In thanks for the lethean river,
  And its endless and mystical roll.

Thank God, I have reached the dark river,
The boundary of all mortal life,
Unbended my bow, and my quiver
Has spent all its arrows of strife,
All its arrows of envy and strife,
And I lay down my bow and my quiver
For beyond the lethean river
They wear not the armor of strife.

Like the over-ripe stock of the harvest,
Awaiting the husbandman's knife,
So I await for the boatman,
And the sound of his light canoe:
Not as I wait for a foeman,
But the clasp of a hand that is true,
To pilot me safely over
Through the mists and clouds that hover,
'Twixt this and the heavenly shore,
The ever bright, love-lighted shore.

THE LOVERS.

Their parting words in anger burned,
Their lips were curled with scorn,
With bitterness and scorn;
And yet their hearts within them yearned,
With loving longing throbbed and burned,
On that September morn.

Haughty and proud, neither would yield,
Though anyone could see,
With half an eye could see,
Their hearts to each were never sealed,
Their very scorn this truth revealed
So plainly unto me.

And yet they parted on that morn,
In manner quite austere,
Quite frigid and severe;
Another hour had not been born
Before each shed, with sigh forlorn,
The penitential tear.

SELF-ADMONITION.

Oh, troubled heart be still, be calm, be brave,
Rise in thy might and prove thine own self strong;
Force back the rising tears and freeze the fount
Of weakness whence they spring, and let no act,
Of either friend or foe, swerve thee one jot
From path which marks the royal way of truth
Unto thyself. Cast from life's troubled barque,
If needs be, everything, save self-respect;
But to this do thou cling as unto hope,
And storms, however fierce, at length will calm,
And skies, however dark, will beam with light,
And sorrow's tears give way to smiles of joy,
And bitter thoughts be turned to thoughts of love.

Pain enters deeper into souls of truth
Than into those that lesser heed her ways.
Virtue full oft receives the crown of thorns,
While, for a season, roses bloom about
The paths of sin, but at the core the worm
Which dieth not, saps every fount of peace
And withers every budding thought of joy,
Eclipsing hope and nourishing despair.

A MESSAGE.

Blow softly, sweet winds, on her brow;
Kiss gently her fair, rosy cheek,
And unto her pearly ear now
Some sweet thought of love gently speak.

Patriotic and Miscellaneous Poems

INDEPENDENCE DAY.

HEROIC deeds make holy days;
  The brightest page of all the years
Is that which to the race displays
  The grandest truth undimmed by fears.
A faith that firmly, boldly stands
  On the eternal rock of Right;
That ceases not in its demands
  For justice, liberty and light!

Faith in the future of mankind,
  Faith in the glory yet to be,
That strengthens, lifts and lights the mind—
  Presaging final victory.
A freedom that shall know no king
  Save justice, when with mercy shown;
That every fetter yet shall fling
  To ocean winds when fiercely blown.

Oh, day! most sacred to the race,
  Oh, day! that gave to Freedom birth;
That thrones of tyrants did displace,
  And all the world with hope did girth;
We greet thee with joy's loud acclaim,
  In anthem grand, and martial song,
We worship Freedom in thy name—
  Immortal enemy of wrong.

Thy emblem, light; its starry folds,
    Borne on the waves of heaven's air;
In it, mankind at last beholds
    The proudest ensign floating there.
Banner of Truth! forever shine,
    Thy staff unmoved shall e'er endure;
Thy radiant glory all divine,
    Shall to the race their rights secure.

Before thy gleams the shades of night,
    Rolled back in terror when the day
Of thy effulgent birth of light
    Made clear to all proud Freedom's way.
The hand of error fell from power;
    Wrong from her citadels was hurled;
Baptized in thy first natal hour,
    Proud day and banner of the world!

Under the guidance of thy stars,
    Man shall attain his highest goal;
No blot his sovereign armor mars,
    Unfettered, free, his mind and soul.
Free to unfold into the light,
    Free to reach upward, on and on;
Free to dispel the shroud of night,
    And chant a welcome to the dawn.

Fill full the bowl and let us drink
    To every hero of the past;
For none beneath the waves should sink,
    Their work complete stands forth at last!
Fill full the bowl, for all divine
    Above us floats against the sky,
"Old Glory," Freedom's spotless sign,
    With spirit that can never die!

Then hail, all hail this sacred hour!
    Wrong meets again its Waterloo;
For here we grasp the prize, the flower—
    Man's brotherhood forever true.
The deeds of martyrs all sublime,
    Of all the ages past are blent,
Whate'er their country or their time,
    In Freedom's perfect monument.

Oh, sons of Poland, rise and sing!
Oh, spirits of Thermopylæ!
For you the glorious plaudits ring,
Though sleeping far beyond the sea;
Awake! arise from your repose,
And join the world's glad jubilee;
Now sweetly blooms your cherished rose—
Man walks the earth unfettered, free!

A wreath! A wreath! Crown every tomb,
Of those who fought in honor's name;
They died that Freedom's flowers might bloom—
Give to them each a deathless fame!
Above the graves where heroes sleep,
Let bloom the sweet forget-me-not,
While nations bow their heads and weep—
With holy tears embalm each spot.

THE SWORD OF GRANT.

Preserve that sword for it shall be,
Through ages yet to come,
A token bright of loyalty
To every peaceful home;
And all shall love it o'er the earth,
As emblem of the matchless worth
Where e'er sweet peace shall roam,
Of him who crowned fair liberty,
With power and strength, in victory.

Preserve it well, it is to-day
The Nation's glorious pride,
Its honor ne'er can fade away,
Through fire it has been tried.
Let roses deck it, and the vine
Around its gleaming blade entwine,
For none on earth beside,
Was drawn with firmer hope to see
Peace rule the world in harmony.

Sacred for aye this gleaming blade,
As Freedom's sacred sod,
By tyrant hands though long delayed,
It voiced the will of God;
As with its glinting flash of steel,
It did sweet liberty reveal,
To those beneath the rod,
Establishing kind heaven's plan;
The noble brotherhood of man.

Preserve it for the noble deeds
Of valor it has done,
Its simple faith unbound by creeds,
Wrought for man's good alone;
'Twas drawn in war that we might see
Peace rule our land in unity,
For this its battles won,
And that sweet peace the land should bless,
With all her joy and gentleness.

A LEADER'S DEATH.

Strike the timbrel, sound the lyre,
Let sad requiems be sung,
The muffled bells be softly tolled,
Let all souls to Heaven aspire
In low and solemn words of prayer,
For the soul of the departed —
For the great life which is no more.
Bury our hero with tenderest care,
Fashion the tomb where his frame shall repose,
Under the willows, and let it be where
The nightingale sings, and bloometh the rose.

Let deep-toned cannon's thunder,
Rend the azure robe asunder,
With their voice of warlike thunder,
As they speak the awful tidings
Of the Nation's stupendous loss;
Fitting it is that "war dogs'" notes
Should echo from their iron throats
A lament o'er his noble tomb;

For when the air was filled with gloom —
With treason's dark and awful gloom —
By his command their wild, fierce boom
Bespoke for treason a short life.
And bore the Nation through the strife
Of civil war, and it arose
Proud conqueror o'er all its foes.
The debt to him the Nation owes
Is all that human power can pay —
On beds of laurel to repose —
To place his name beyond decay.
To write on each and every heart,
In words of bright and glowing flame,
The greatness of his matchless name;
Embalm in story and in song,
How for the right and 'gainst the wrong
He wrought with superhuman skill,
Surpassing with his iron will
And wondrous judgment, all the deeds
Achieved by man, whate'er the creeds
Which urged them on ; his holy plan
Was to exemplify in man
The right which since the world began
Had been denied — the right to be
A man, untrammeled, upright, free.

Mourn, for the warrior is no more;
Mourn, for the statesman is no more;
Mourn, for the soldier lieth prone;
Mourn, for the citizen is gone.
His like we shall not look upon,
Though millions rise and pass away;
Though there should come a brighter day,
No man can on the scroll of fame
Emblazon a more glorious name;
Of deeds heroic, none can be
Of higher, loftier degree
Than those he did amid the storm,
When flowed the life blood fresh and warm
From out the Nation's bleeding form.

THE OLD MAN'S REQUEST.

Let me rest where you will, the only condition
    I attach to the choice of a place for my tomb,
Be it where my loved wife—God bless her devotion—
    May rest when her life shall eternally bloom;
Fan her gently I pray, ye soft winds of heaven,
    Oh, peaceful and calm may her life's river e'er glide,
For each sorrow a balm, oh, let it be given,
    When life's journey be o'er let her rest by my side.

Through sunshine and storm of life's checkered voyage,
    The soul of my being—my life's guiding star,
Devoted companion to soothe and encourage,
    My solace in peace and my goddess in war;
When alone there remains the beautiful casket,
    When the spirit of life shall have flown from my bride,
Remember my prayer—in love's name I ask it,
    Let her rest, sweetly rest in peace by my side.

Let her rest by my side when the light of her glory
    In the sunset of life shall grow dim 'till it fade,
When life's chapter be closed, and ended the story,
    Let her dust with my dust in silence be laid;
She hath shared with me long life's pain and its pleasure,
    The light of my soul, since I kissed her my bride;
Hath filled all my life with sweet joy in full measure,
    When her night cometh on let her rest by my side.

INJUSTICE OF IDLENESS.

All days of idleness are brought to one
    By throwing on some other double weight;
For never since our parents' woes begun
    Has oped, on earth, a Paradisal gate.

All here are called to labor, and the road
    Is measured from the cradle to the grave;
If so, through life some bear a lighter load,
    Their honor, then, is less in being brave.

THE SWORD OF WALLACE.

Sword of Wallace, how we love it,
None more brightly shone above it,
None was truer to its trust;
None was braver in endeavor,
Treason's grasp to quickly sever,
Let it proudly shine for ever,
Free from time's destroying rust;
'Tis of him a true reminder,
There was never yet a kinder
Heart consigned to mother dust.

Sheathe it proudly, as he wore it,
Sheathe it bravely, as he bore it,
Emblem true of loyalty;
First in battle line defending,
First amid the traitors wending,
Where the Blue with Grey were blending;
In the struggle there to see,
That the cause of right was winning,
Over hosts of rebels sinning,
'Gainst the banner of the free.

Sheathe that glinting sword of battle,
For no more the din and rattle
Of the conflict now is heard;
For its flag, behold, is streaming,
Over heroes who lie dreaming,
Where its powerful stroke was gleaming,
For the right—his chosen word,
As it struck the foe with terror,
Free from cowardice and error,
It is Freedom's glorious sword.

THE WARRIOR'S DEATH.

Life's battle wanes apace at last;
Lo! in the West its setting sun
Gives way, and shadows dim are cast,
Which tell the warrior's work is done;
Upon his brow
A smile plays uow,
Telling the final vict'ry's won.

THE LONG ROLL IS BEATING.

The long roll is beating, haste, haste to the battle,
  The boom of the batteries' thunders enlarge,
The sharp ringing sound of the musketry's rattle
  Nerved every brave heart to the call of the charge.
        Into the crash
        With sudden dash
They met the rebel's haughty line,
        Causing to reel
        Their blades of steel,
And lower foul treason's flaunting sign.

Charge! heroes, charge! for the life of the Nation
  Now hangs in the balance, 'tis yours to declare,
Whether the hope of your father's creation
  Shall flourish in peace or now die in despair;
        Up every arm,
        Preserve it from harm
And hurl back the foe to its doom;
        Paint all the ground
        With blood as you wound,
And dig for vile treason a tomb.

Let the air tremble with sounds of your waking,
  And see that the foe shall inhale with each breath
The poisons of woe that treason is making;
  Let them drink to its dregs the wine of its death.
        Brew well the cup,
        And fill it up
With treason's hemlock juice of hell,
        And let them drink,
        Then quickly sink
Into the grave they digged so well.

Gallantly forward, swift up from the river,
  Moved the great columns of blue-coats into line;
Resolving that death, and death only, should sever
  Their will from their purpose—a purpose divine.
        That nothing should mar
        The gleam of a star,
Nor one from their banner be torn;
        Though wars should increase
        And murder sweet peace,
The stars all as one must be borne.

"*E pluribus unum*" the key of their song,
"The union forever" the echoes replied;
As through the deep forest it thundered along,
Forever in one as the waves of the tide.
In union is strength,
In breadth and in length
Our country unsevered shall be;
Its stars shall e'er shine
With pure ray divine
From sky of its banner so free.

THE CALL TO ARMS.

Hark to the voice of your country now calling
For aid in subduing her traitorous foes,
Who have fired on her flag, oh treason appalling!
Rush quick to her rescue, resent their foul blows.

Fly to her standard, no time for delaying,
The sound of disloyalty's murderous band
Is heard through the hills, her honor betraying,
While treason is spreading all over the land.

Fly to her standard, the long roll is beating,
Haste, haste, keep the old flag still high in the air,
Hurl from her temples, in terror retreating,
All those who would stain her fair loyalty there.

See them come flocking from peaceful homes breaking
And casting their all at their loved country's feet;
Her cry of distress their manliness waking,
To win back her honor or die in defeat.

Hark to the music, "Columbia" is ringing
A call to her sons, to the loyal and brave;
See them march on, each true heart bravely singing
The Union forever or rest in the grave.

A ROYAL LEGACY.

My father was a kindly man,
Of massive, stalwart frame,
And when to speak I first began,
It was to lisp his name;
And in my mind I yet can see
His face, as my first memory.

His look was such a searching one,
Shot from his piercing eye,
As he would say to me: " My son,
Your country ne'er deny."
I often wondered why he said:
"That is a message from the dead."

Above the mantel hung his sword,
Sheathed in a well-worn case;
I can remember every word
That found on it a place:
" For God, for Honor, and for Power,"
Entwined with vine, and leaf, and flower.

And just above, with pinions spread,
And poised as if for flight,
An eagle's form, though still and dead,
A grand, imposing sight;
His talons grasping firm and bold
A shield and arrows tipped with gold.

About the bird, in folds of light,
The banner of the free
Completed that most stirring sight —
A glorious trinity!
In which was power to stir the blood
Of loyalty's great brotherhood!

"Come hither, son," my father said,
When we two were alone;
His countenance to thought was wed,
And solemn was his tone,
As taking down that flashing sword,
He bade me heed his every word.

"My son," he said, "this sword is mine,
It was thy grandsire's, boy,
And it in turn will soon be thine;
See that no rust alloy
Or tarnish its bright, glinting steel,
While thou hast power to think and feel.

"This sword has hewn the way to peace,
Through many bloody frays,
And may its power for right increase,
With increase of thy days;
Thy sire's, thy grandsire's honor, too,
I give, to guard with this, to you.

"Swear, boy, that while thou hast a breath
That flag thou wilt sustain,
And bravely choose a soldier's death,
Rather than treason's stain
Should dim the glitter of its stars,
Or trail in dust its shining bars."

Now sire with grandsire is at rest,
And yet they live to-day,
Their loyal spirits in this breast
Rule with a fervent sway;
To touch that sword is e'er to hear
Clearly resounding in my ear:

"'For God, for Honor, and for Power,'
This motto ever keep,
And if, perchance, should come the hour,
Bid every feeling sleep,
Save that the hope of all the world
Is that our flag be kept unfurled."

THE DISASTER OF JOHNSTOWN.

All day o'er the city of Johnstown,
The sun, like an emblem of love,
Had brilliantly lighted that valley
And Peace, like a white-wingéd dove,
Dispelled every thought of disaster;
No cloud came to mar the sweet dream
Of this valley which lay in the mountains
Asleep by the murmuring stream.

The sound of the forge and the bellows
Was heard floating out on the air;
The laughter of children that sported
Unfettered by sorrow or care;
The mill with the sound of its grinding,
All over the valley was heard,
And out from the orchards came floating
The sweet notes of the warbling bird.

All nature seemed full of rejoicing,
The stream through the valley along,
A lullaby sang to that city —
A sweet and ineffable song;
The mountains looked down so benignly,
For now their great shadows were cast,
As if they would shroud the sweet valley
In dark, mystical realms at last.

Hark! lo, a wild horseman is coming,
As though to a hurricane wed;
His face it is ashen and pallid
As though 'twere the face of the dead;
His hair is disheveled and flying,
By winds madly fanned in his speed;
With lash and with spur he is urging
Still swifter his noble bay steed.

His voice echoes over the valley,
"Flee, flee to the hills for your lives!
The lake has burst out of its bondage,
Flee, flee, ere the torrent arrives!"

Swift on down the valley he passes,
To warn all the people of harm,
His voice bearing earnest conviction
And filling each breast with alarm.

The people rush out of their dwellings
To see the wild horseman go by,
But few of them heeded his warning—
"What means he," they ask, "by this cry?"
One moment they waited, inquiring,
Then came down the valley a sound
Like a mighty battle of thunders,
While trembled affrighted the ground.

Then came a great wall of black waters,
So fierce in its wild, maddened course
That it crushed all things in the valley
With its mighty and terrible force.
Trees swayed like the grass in the tempest,
And houses were hurled in the air,
While Death rode the waves of the deluge
And spoke to each heart of despair.

The billows reached out in their anger
And shouted to valley and hill:
"We demand every one for our vengeance,
No power can withstand our strong will.
Bring every fond father and mother,
And every pure babe and sweet child;
Not one of them all shall escape us,
With vengeance alone we are wild.

"For I, the great spirit of waters,
Have spoken my edict in power,
That death shall rule over this valley,
His reign be complete in an hour.
All those who pay tribute to Mammon,
All those who are servants of God,
Not one of them all shall escape me,
Whose feet in this valley have trod."

The call of these murderous waters,
None heard but were bound to obey;
All hell in its fury came rushing
Along with the waters that day.
Sweet, innocent babes, from the bosoms
Of mothers were ruthlessly torn,
And away by the black, rushing demons
To death and destruction were borne.

Strong men were dry reeds in its fury,
Tossed hither and thither at will;
Its craving for life was appalling,
Its desire alone was to kill.
It seized the fair maids in their beauty,
With strength of unmeasured desire,
And proved its deep passions far greater
Than all of the demons of fire.

It kissed madly their cheeks, and the roses
Were instantly faded and gone;
The pallor of death, like dull ashes,
Lay over them all as though one.
It toyed with their beautiful tresses,
Alike with the dark and the fair;
Laughed loudly in mocking derision
At cry of their wailing despair.

All death seemed that day in the waters
And chose in this valley where bloom
Was fairest and purest, most lovely,
To make for its victims a tomb.
Oh, God! when the waters receded,
What a sight was there to behold!
The fair and the weak and the mighty
Of earth, on its bosom lay cold!

The flame of truth burns bright and strong,
The world is dazzled by its rays;
A pæan grand bursts from the throng,
An anthem of devoutest praise.
And here aloft, kissing the sky,
The starry banner is unfurled,
Revealing unto every eye
The hope and light of all the world.

Behind us lie the shades of night,
Before, the bright, eternal morn;
Each moment yields a new delight,
Each day a higher trust is born.
The faith of yesterday, to-day
Is turned to knowledge, and we rise,
Testing the truth of prophecy
In light of new discoveries.

The faith that ruled the Spaniard bold,
And drew him westward o'er the seas,
Is current coin to-day. Behold,
The need of greater argosies!
However bright the light may shine,
However radiant bursts the dawn:
Darkness the shores beyond entwine,
And Hope still whispers "on and on!"

The winds blow fierce, the waves dash high;
Life is an ocean deep and wide;
Death strews the way, its victims lie
Helpless upon the heaving tide.
"Watchman, ahoy! What of the night?
Gleams there no sign of coming dawn?"
"Yes, Captain, yes; there is one light —
The star of Hope shines brightly on."

The waves grow rougher day by day;
All that we are, or strive to be,
Is now required to sail the way
To mankind's final destiny.
"Man overboard!" Quick! lend a hand,
He must not sink beneath the wave;
Accursed would be the harbor land
If reached by a neglect to save!

Sail on! sail on, brave hearts, sail on!
Though tempests rage and billows roar;
For idle hands there comes no dawn,
Work balms the aching to the core.
Sail on! sail on! tread firm the deck,
Shout loud the song, nor pause to weep;
To the brave heart can come no wreck —
He will provide His servants sleep.

THE CHARGE.

Hark to the bugle's stirring blast,
The rolling of the drum,
The shouting of the loud command;
The charging foe, they come!
And like a wild, fierce hurricane,
With clouds surcharged with deadly rain,
They strike the listener dumb,
As with their deadly missiles there
They fill and blacken all the air.

Now rolls the seething tempest high,
Its thunders rend the sky!
At every burning, scorching flash,
Stern echoings reply,
Then dashes doubly fierce again
The life-destroying hail and rain,
Which human power defy,
For every flash and thunder tone,
Claims countless victims for its own.

OCTOBER HILLS.

A silver vail hangs o'er the wooded hills
And curtains out the kisses of the sun;
'Neath the green forest bowers, the tiny rills,
With measured flow, to low-voiced music run;
The wild bird's notes, of sweet melodious song,
Flow like a stream of melody along.

The scarlet leaves with listless motion fall,
Wavering through the air with scarce a sound;
Silence, like magic, broodeth over all,
The air is motionless as is the ground.
The long and polished needles of the pines,
No longer tremulous, are still as death;
No fern or blade of grass sways or inclines
As is their wont, to Zephyr's faintest breath.

The sky a perfect canopy o'erhead,
And drooping all about, its folds of blue
Seem nearer drawn, than where the lowlands spread
From morning's waking sun, 'til evening's dew;
While here and there a fragile gleam of mist,
Seems like a bit of Summer's bridal veil,
Torn from her train, and by the sunbeams kissed
To sky-seas for some Sunsprite's barque a sail.

FORGIVENESS.

And it is best while yet we live,
To heal all heartaches and forgive.
For life at best is but a span
Wherein the grandest, noblest man
Is he who gives to one and all
Forgiveness unconditional.

Forgiveness, oh! the holy balm,
No word so sweet from human tongue;
Life's bitter storm becomes a calm
As flows its healing sound among
The waves of woe, which constant rise
To blot the sun from out our skies.

THE CHRISTMAS TREE.

Oh! fair are the boughs of the Christmas tree,
And rich are the fruits that they bear;
No good of the land or the rolling sea,
No matter where or however it be,
But are found to be growing there.
Then welcome all,
At Christmas call,
Let the glad chimes ring with glee,
And drive away,
All care to-day,
While we dance round the Christmas tree.

Let the proud ships sail from over the main,
And may all of the winds be fair;
And bring of their stores to the tree again,
From Alaska's shores and the isles of Spain,
Of the wealth which they have to spare.
The Christmas tree
To-day shall be,
The richest that ever grew;
No wind shall blow,
No river flow,
But shall add to its wealth anew.

Let the divers plunge to the ocean caves,
Where the royal Sea-king's jewels are,
Unlocking the grasp of the white-capped waves,
Which have held the gems from the eyes of knaves,
With a greater than miser's care.
From every store
We most adore,
Of its wealth be gathered free,
For I declare,
No jewel rare,
Is too good for the Christmas tree.

From the palmy isles of the Southern seas,
From the vaults of eternal snow;
From the matin winds to the vesper breeze,
From the heights of lands to the depths of seas

Let messengers speedily go,
And quickly bring
Their offering,
And the crown for each one shall be,
The matchless prize
Of loving eyes,
That are charmed by the Christmas tree.

In a precious soil grows the Christmas tree,
In the hearts of the good and true;
'Tis the hands of love and of sympathy,
That deck all its branches so lavishly,
With the gifts which they freely strew.
The joy it gives
Forever lives,
And the world will the better be,
For the love and light,
So pure and bright,
That beams from the Christmas tree.

ELIJAH AND THE RAVENS.

By the lonely brook of Chereth,
Sat God's servant in a cave,
Naught of comfort or of blessing
Save alone its sparkling wave;
For the earth was all a desert,
Famine, famine everywhere;
Gone was fruit, and flower, and blossom,
Hungry was the desert air.

But in God the prophet trusted,
Trusted all things to His hand,
Feared not famine, feared no evil,
In this waste and desert land;
Laid firm hold upon His promise,
Trusted fully in His word,
And though human power forsook him,
Yet his faith was firm, unstirred.

Hunger preyed upon his system,
   Famine stared him in the face.
Yet he murmurs, "all sufficient
   Is God's bounteous power and grace;"
Patiently he waits God's coming,
   Asks not when, or how, or why,
Only trusting, fully trusting,
   Fearing not to live or die.

See, there comes a flock of ravens,
   Circling o'er him in the sky,
Flutt'ring nearer, nearer, nearer,
   With their weird peculiar cry;
Can this be of good an omen?
   Can they aught portend of good?
Behold, his simple faith is honored,
   Lo, the ravens bring him food.

LOVE'S TRIBUTE.

The heart that beat with joy and pride
   Is now forever still,
The winsome, gay and lovely bride
   A narrow grave has filled.

The gladsome smile, the loving voice,
   Are seen and heard no more;
Her presence that did all rejoice
   Is gone for evermore.

Let sorrow weave her deepest shade,
   And softly shed her tears;
Let flowers be gathered, wreaths to braid
   By hands her love endears.

Let every tribute earth can pay
   Do honor to her now,
From every floweret cull a spray
   To deck her lovely brow.

WAYSIDE PLEASURES.

When worn and weary with life's heavy load,
Our fainting hearts have been revived and cheered
By cooling draughts of sweetest sympathy.
Full oft, when troubled waves rolled high and fierce
Have kindly hands poured out the oil of peace,
And calm, blue skies have arched and smiled serene,
Where angry clouds of storm have fiercely blown,
And pleasant plains of peace have oft appeared
Where rugged mountains rose to bar our way.
In arid deserts fragrant flowers have bloomed,
And sweet, fresh grasses grown to cheer our way;
Oft from our hearts the piercing thorns of pain
By tender hands have been withdrawn with care,
And hours of gloom been lit with joy and love.

WHAT DAME RUMOR SAID.

The morn was bright, the month was June,
  When with my line and rod,
Humming a gay and cheerful tune,
  The mountain path I trod.
The dashing stream was cool and clear,
  As swiftly on it sped,
Filled with fine trout that knew no fear,
  So false Dame Rumor said.

From out my book the tempting flies,
  With care I quickly chose;
And angled for a finny prize,
  But never one arose.
Dame Rumor'd led me to believe,
  That here no fly could fall,
But trout so easy to deceive,
  Would swallow line and all!

I fished all day until the night,
And caught one tiny trout;
Its size so small, its weight so light,
Scarce moved my line about.
With lagging steps and rueful sighs,
I left the fishing grounds;
Dame Rumor said I'd caught a prize,
Which weighed nigh seven pounds!

My friends next day all sought the stream,
And angled with a will,
Eager at morning's early gleam,
Their baskets all to fill.
At night when they returned to town,
All looked at me askance;
On every brow a darkling frown,
Lightning in every glance.

And now each one I chance to meet,
With injured air goes by;
Which in the club or on the street,
Says plainly, "Sir, you lie."
Or, with derision's baneful look,
The hint goes all the rounds;
"He caught the trout with line and hook,
That weighed nigh seven pounds!"

INDEPENDENCE.

So live that thine own soul within
May catch and hold the sweets of life;
Those may deceive thee who have been
Friends in the hours of darkest strife.

Let not thine anger on them dwell,
Deem them as dead, though living yet;
Think on loved scenes, and Beauty's spell
Will banish from thy mind regret.

THE STRUGGLE FOR BREAD.

But one cruse of oil, and one measure of meal,
And the wife lying sick in the bed;
No wonder the chills o'er the husband's heart steal,
As the future looms up black with dread.
The bright star of hope, o'er a sea of despair,
Glows faint in the gathering gloom;
The clouds by the tempest are hurled through the air,
And roll their black forms through the room.

Their pledge of affection — fond, cherished first-born —
Is heard in the darkness to cry;
It pierces his heart, as the thought comes that morn
Will even a dry crust deny.
The wind at the casement now pipes forth a wail,
A howl in the distance is heard,
And borne to his ears on the wings of the gale,
The cry of an ominous bird.

The vicious wolves gather while rageth the storm,
Fierce gleam their white fangs through the night;
They leap in their madness all over his form,
And tear at his throat gleaming white.
With strength of a Sampson, spurred on by true love,
He dashes their forms from the door;
Great God, in Thy mercy, look down from above,
And aid in their struggles the poor.

The land has of fatness enough and to spare,
But the misers have garnered it all,
And deaf are their hearts, as the storm-beaten air,
To those who in wretchedness call.
The light that emblazons our banner so fair,
And justice proclaims to the world,
Shines on stricken hearts that are doomed to despair,
Though their honor has never been furled.

DIANA'S DEFEAT.

Hark! through the woods the winding horn,
And baying of the hounds is heard;
Affrighted from their feast at morn,
Flee every timid beast and bird.

"Who dares disturb our wild retreat?"
The Elfins and the Dryads cry;
"Who comes with footfalls strong, and fleet
As wind-waves from a stormy sky?

"'Tis she, the goddess of the chase,
Diana, with her trailing hounds;
No other dare invade this place —
No other knows these pathless grounds."

The Water-nymphs within the stream
Gather at call of their fair queen;
They feel their duty is supreme
To stand, the hounds and game between.

On comes the fleet, affrighted deer,
Pursued by huntress and by hounds;
Trembling from flight and awful fear,
Into the stream the stag now bounds.

Boldly the Water-nymphs appear,
Their bravery none can deny,
For 'neath Diana's poiséd spear,
They shout defiantly this cry:

"Hold! but the shore the gods thee gave,
We will protect the hunted deer;
Its refuge is the gleaming wave;
Stand back! for we are masters here."

A GLIMPSE OF SPRING.

There are blooms upon the cherry,
There's an odor in the air,
And the robin's song so merry
Tells of gladness everywhere;
There's a golden sheen of glory
Clothing all the joyous scene,
And the grasses tell the story
Of their birth, so fresh and green.

How the swallows sail and twitter
At their work about the eaves,
When the morning sunbeams glitter
On the jewels of the leaves;
See how busy at their labors,
Bringing mud and bits of straw,
Chatting gaily with their neighbors,
Each unto itself a law.

WRONG IS OF NIGHT.

Mortality doth shroud the soul
As darkness veils the world at night,
And we, at best, can only see
A glimmer of the distant stars,
And this enough to prove that we
Shall know the light when glorious morn
Shall with its sweet effulgence break
Upon our sight, and all around
Shall know the light, and feel the truth,
To be a part of each one's soul,
Wherein is found no taint of wrong,
For wrong is of the night alone,
And all of evil is confined
Beneath its darkened canopy.

HAIL, BROTHER, HAIL.

Hail, brother, hail! how farest thou?
    Long years have passed since last we met;
The frosts of Time are on thy brow,
    Life's sun for us inclines to set.

How hast thou found the road of life?
    Have peace and love enshrined thy path,
Or have the angry clouds of strife
    Burst o'er thee with their flames of wrath?

Has life proved what in youth it seemed,
    When gilded with Hope's radiant morn?
Have flow'rs proved sweet as thou hadst dreamed,
    Or hath each rose disclosed a thorn?

Dost thou remember how as boys
    We dreamed and planned, as all boys will,
Of all the bright and blissful joys
    We thought our future life would fill?

Come sit thee by this running stream,
    While life doth flow like it away,
And tell me if to thee it seem
    Another stream with which to play?

What thinkest thou of time and change,
    Are seen things real, or no, I pray?
Is it not dreamland, the whole range
    Encompassed by the light of day?

Is form and matter, force and weight,
    But the resultant of a will?
Can we know aught beyond this state,
    Where we are grain for Time's old mill?

Doth all life flow into a sea—
    A waveless, stagnant sea of death?
Is there no immortality,
    No life beyond this fleeting breath?

"Yes, brother, yes, I feel and know
That life is other than a dream;
It will forever onward flow,
And flowing on, still brighter gleam.

"The constant efforts of the soul,
To free itself from bars of time,
Proves its desire to reach its goal —
A brighter, better, fairer clime."

MY OLD DUCK-CALL.

I was feeling through the pockets
Of my cast-off corduroys,
Such as we, you will remember,
Used to wear when we were boys.
As I searched my hunting jacket,
Something from its pocket fell,
Which, if blessed with revelation,
Could some wondrous stories tell.

It was made of hardened cherry,
And o'er my primitive decoys
It had brought the wary "flappers"
From a distance with its noise;
So that as they sailed above us,
We would rise and blaze away,
'Til the evening shadows gathered
At the closing of the day.

Gods! the hunts upon the marshes,
How the pleasures I recall,
You, and I, and little Fannie
Used to revel in each Fall,
Where the wild-rice grew in freedom
On the river's bayous thick,
Where to bag the ducks by dozens
Was a very easy trick.

Then I sat me down reflecting,
  On those times of long ago,
And my thoughts were very pleasant,
  Such as only sportsmen know;
For they spoke of joys unmeasured,
  Such as only youths can feel,
When down on the river bottoms,
  Waiting for the ducks, they kneel.

I recalled the vivid picture,
  When one Autumn afternoon
You had wounded with the rifle,
  At long range, a diving loon;
And how Fannie sought to fetch him
  From the bosom of the lake,
And of how he fought like Satan,
  With his kingdom for a stake.

How you thought you'd end the battle,
  Creeping out upon a log
Where a moccasin lay sunning,
  And you jumped into the bog!
How you swore and raved and sputtered,
  And fierce threatened me with lead,
When I laughed and shouted loudly
  When we found the snake was dead.

Now I feel the young blood coursing
  Swiftly through my sluggish veins,
And I feel my old heart beating
  As my soul its youth regains;
For the calendar is pointing
  To the sombre months of Fall,
I must try my skill at shooting—
  Use once more the old duck-call.

UNDER THE GREENWOOD TREE.

(Dedicated to the COUNTRY CLUB of San Francisco.)

Under the green and leafy boughs
Of the old greenwood tree,
Are joys no other spot allows,
So fresh, so pure and free.

CHORUS:

Under the greenwood tree, my boys,
Under the greenwood tree;
Elsewhere there may be sweeter joys,
But they are not for me.

When Spring her robe of beauty spreads,
O'er mountain, vale, and lea;
There is no spot where beauty weds
Like to the greenwood tree.

CHORUS:

Under the greenwood tree, my boys,
Under the greenwood tree;
Elsewhere there may be sweeter joys,
But they are not for me.

There wild birds build, and mate, and sing,
And all life gambols free;
No nimble foot or sailing wing
But loves the greenwood tree.

CHORUS:

Under the greenwood tree, my boys,
Under the greenwood tree;
Elsewhere there may be sweeter joys,
But they are not for me.

Ho, ho! ho, ho! we shout and sing,
And laugh right merrily,
And on the air our glad notes fling,
From underneath the tree.

CHORUS:

Under the greenwood tree, my boys,
  Under the greenwood tree;
Elsewhere there may be sweeter joys,
  But they are not for me.

The freedom which its shelter gives
  Is that of high degree,
For there one truly, freely lives,
  Under the greenwood tree.

CHORUS:

Under the greenwood tree, my boys,
  Under the greenwood tree;
Elsewhere there may be sweeter joys,
  But they are not for me.

Then welcome all from toil and care,
  Who would be gay and free,
Come breathe the pure and fragrant air
  Which fans beneath the tree.

CHORUS:

Under the greenwood tree my boys,
  Under the greenwood tree;
Elsewhere there may be sweeter joys,
  But they are not for me.

A LITTLE PRINCESS.

I know a winsome bit of light,
　　Who sunshine carries everywhere;
Who is her mama's chief delight,
　　Bringing her joy without a care.

If you could see her great, brown eyes,
　　And catch the glinting of her hair,
You would exclaim in great surprise:
　　"She is all sweetness, I declare!"

She never yet was known to cry,
　　Nor naughty be one single hour;
And none who know her will deny
　　The magic sweetness of her pow'r.

She is a little lady quite,
　　So neat and pretty, sweet and good;
Her garments all of purest white
　　From dainty slipper to her hood.

And everybody loves her well,
　　Some for herself, but I mistake
If many more the truth would tell:
　　They love her for her mama's sake.

But she is sweet and cute, I vow,
　　I would just dearly love to shake her;
She is a doll, I must allow,
　　This Princess Helen Wilber-Baker.

TWO CENTRAL POINTS.

Stranger, from whence and whither bound?
　　He said, "I have but left my home;
All roads lead there, I've ever found,
　　And from thence lead, for me, to Rome."

MOUNTAIN PLEASURES.

Who says that a trip to the mountains,
Away from the marts and their din,
Is not as the stream of salvation
Compared to the highways of sin ?

Just let him stand forth and affirm it —
If such an one there should here be ;
I'll vouch for the fact that his nature
To cleanse would exhaust the deep sea.

One who, in invisible water,
Forever is washing his hands,
And plying his cunning devices
All over the seas and the lands.

Who, with gay colored net of seduction,
Casts ever to catch whom he can ;
An enemy, selfish and tireless,
A foe unto God and to man.

For who can love God or His creatures,
Unless he loves God's work alone,
Where His revelations, unchanging,
Are written in rivers and stone ?

A trip to the Upper Sierras
Gives one a broad view — above creeds,
Of that which the Master has written
Concerning man's innermost needs.

A sermon in each laughing brooklet ;
An anthem in each foaming stream ;
Each mountain a symbol of glory,
From which benign blessings e'er gleam.

Alone with God's work ! How it solemns
And leads the faint heart to the brink
Of life's flowing river of sweetness,
While whisper God's angels : "Drink, drink."

ALPHA AND OMEGA.

The years sweep on; Time knows not rest nor sleep;
Unwearied and perpetual his speed;
In calm or storm his mighty steeds move on,
Grinding beneath his chariot wheels all things
That are, into a dust impalpable.
He seems a god of many whims and moods,
Requiring all of change that is to please
His fancy and to satisfy his soul.
With lute of lively breathing calls he forth,
From out the southland where the palm trees wave,
When wooed to motion by spice-laden airs,
The merry blossom-circled maiden fair,
Who to the measure of his music trips,
With many changing steps, to please his whims.
Her magic wand she waves, and lo! the birds
Of song and beauty circle round her nigh,
Singing in harmony with his gay lute,
While blossoms burst from vine and spreading tree,
And all the air is laden with their sweets.

This pleasantry a season satisfies,
And then his music grows more sweet and low,
When Summer, with an air of dignity
And graces matronly, appears, serene
And calm, as certain of her course and work.
Anon, to slow and measured music, comes
The bronzed and rosy Autumn, bending low
Beneath her fruits — rich promises fulfilled.
When, weary of feasting and of fatness,
Time changes yet again his notes and plays
Of fierceness, flood and storm, of cold and death,
When Winter, breathing sickles sharp and keen,

Sweeps o'er the scene, destroying every sign
Imprinted by this trio of fair queens;
And this is all: hope, labor, reaping, death!

Time watches o'er the cradle of each birth,
And dallies with our infancy, and weaves
A magic wreath which, wooed to fragrant bloom,
Clothes all our future with a livery,
Gorgeous and beautiful unto the eye.
Adown this vista of the future years
Appears the smooth and pleasant path of peace,
Winding beneath umbrageous forests cool,
Where sparkling fountains play and sweet birds sing,
Forming a perfect paradise, wherein
No serpents, seeming, ever can intrude.

Time early weds our infancy to Hope,
And never has he known a sweeter bride—
Fair sister she of Immortality.
On placing our young hand within her palm
He whispers: "She will ever be thy friend,
Cleave unto her as unto life. Give heed
Each moment of thy way unto her voice,
And thou shalt reap thy soul's most fond desire."
Dear Hope! How fair her form! How sweet her smile!
How luminous and bright her wondrous eyes!
How auspicious the journey when begun!
A little way and Grief beside a grave
Throws over our young heart a grewsome awe,
That ever hangs about us on the way,
And Sorrow follows closely, draped in tears.

What weight has grief, or pain, or ills, or woe?
What matters if the sun, with scorching ray,
Beats down upon our unprotected head,

And withers every leaf and verdured blade,
Making of blooming gardens deserts wild?
Doth not Hope beckon on with winning smile?
Doth she not point to honor and to fame?
Holds she not in her hands a jewelled crown,
A wand, and health, and length of days, and love?
Doth she not say: "These are for you, press on?"
The way grows rough and slippery to the feet,
Yawning chasms, seemingly bottomless,
Fall away to darkness on either hand
Of our perilous way, which now becomes
A source of abject terror and affright;
The wind blows fierce; the rain in torrents falls;
The lightning blinds the sight, and thunders roll
With terror-waking detonations near,
And reverberating through the gorges wild
Which are, we dimly see by lightning's gleam,
Strewn thickly with the bruised and mangled forms
Of countless wretches who have fallen here;
Swerve but a hair's breadth from the narrow way,
And all will end in darkness and despair.

Just here, with piercing shriek, a brother slips;
He clings with strength of wild despair, clutching
The narrow shelving of our path, and swings
Over the wall of the great precipice!
Horror depicted on his face, he calls,
In tones of deepest anguish, for our aid;
Our terror-frozen limbs refuse to stir;
Our lips are speechless, and our eyes grow dim;
A faintness creeps into our heart and stills
Its beating, as we sway toward the chasm!
Instinctively our hands clasp those that cling,
When lo! we find our brother and his load,

Added unto our own, doth lighten all!
We lift the fallen to the path again,
And through a rift within the rolling clouds
Streams an effulgent burst of light, which falls
Upon our path to guide and cheer our way.
Fame comes not here, but joy doth fill our soul;
And Mercy whispers: "Peace, brave heart, well done."

This is the acme of all striving here,
The royal robe, the magic wand, the crown;
All else is fleeting as the years, as vain
And unsubstantial as the rainbow's gleam.
Our limbs grow weary and our hearts more weak,
As with a pale and mellow light the day
Fades slowly from the mist-draped evening sky.
Ashes of hopes within the bosom lie,
Where Sorrow sits beside a sepulcher,
Scanning the record of the past, through tears.
The vista groweth dark and darker still,
As fade the mortal senses — sight and sound;
But there, piercing the gloom, shines one bright star,
Sweet Hope, forever dear, forever bright,
Forever leading up and on, and on.
The struggle ceases, all is calm and still;
The star's light flickers faint and dim. How cold!
A shudder gently moves our weary frame;
The shadows deepen and still closer creep;
Our pale lips move a little, murmuring:
"Come Euthanasia! Father, thy spirit.....
Light for our pathway; more light, still more light!"

www.ingramcontent.com/pod-product-compliance
Lightning Source LLC
Chambersburg PA
CBHW021124270326
41929CB00009B/1033
* 9 7 8 3 7 4 3 3 2 8 8 4 6 *